The NPR Curious Listener's Guide to

Jazz

The NPR Curious Listener's Guide to

Jazz

LOREN SCHOENBERG

A Grand Central Press Book

A Perigee Book

A Perigee Book
Published by The Berkley Publishing Group
A division of Penguin Putnam Inc.
375 Hudson Street
New York, New York 10014

PRODUCED BY GRAND CENTRAL PRESS
Paul Fargis, Director
Judy Pray, Executive Editor
Nick Viorst, Series Editor

NATIONAL PUBLIC RADIO
Murray Horwitz, Vice-President, Cultural Programming
Andy Trudeau, Executive Producer, Cultural Programming
Barbara A. Vierow, Project Manager, Business Development
Kate Elliott, Project Manager, Business Development

Copyright © 2002 by Grand Central Press and National Public Radio
Text design by Tiffany Kukec
Cover art by Dan Baxter
Cover design by Jill Boltin

First edition: August 2002

Visit our website at www.penguinputnam.com

Library of Congress Cataloging-in-Publication Data

Schoenberg, Loren, 1958–
The NPR curious listener's guide to Jazz / Loren Schoenberg.
p. cm.
Includes discography, bibliographical references, and index.
ISBN 0-399-52794-X
1. Jazz—History and criticism. I. Title: National Public Radio curious listener's
guide to jazz. II. National Public Radio (U.S.) III. Title.
ML3506 .S34 2002
781.65—dc21   2002025787

Printed in the United States of America

10 9 8 7 6 5 4 3 2 1

Contents

Acknowledgments

This book has been long in coming. It is the result of the last twenty-five years I have spent in New York as a Jazz musician. Jazz is more times than not a supremely collaborative effort, and I like to think of this book in the same way. Of the untold hours of conversation about the music and everything related to it, many insights that friends shared with me came back during the writing of this book. Going back a ways, Harold Ashby, Eddie Durham, Jo Jones, Dick Katz, Barbara Lea, Jack Bradley, Benny Goodman, Hank Jones, Ruby Braff, Sylvia Syms, Mel Lewis, Dick Sudhalter, Albert Murray, Howard McGhee, Bobby Short, Artie Shaw, John Lewis, Jean Bach, Gunther Schuller, Martin Williams, Bill Triglia, and Dave Schildkraut all gave me the great gift of their time and wisdom.

During the gestation of this book, there were many times

when Mark Lopeman, Jon Gordon, Brent Wallarab, Dick Katz, Ken Peplowski, Allen Lowe, Billy Taylor, and Steve Wilson were available for as long as needed to talk through potentially thorny issues.

My editor, Nick Viorst, showed supreme patience and should be a psychologist on top of his already first-rate literary skills.

Thanks especially to Tadao Yasutomi for his steadfast support. Three close and longtime friends whose support and guidance have been vital in the sphere of becoming my own intellectual being (and in the more practical word-to-word sense, too) are Dan Morgenstern, Stanley Crouch, and Edward Berger.

Finally, to my parents, Bob and Evelyn Schoenberg, who made everything possible for my life in the arts, most significantly through those long, early stretches when it seemed as though as I may not have been knocking at the right door.

Loren Schoenberg

Foreword

by Wynton Marsalis

Curiosity is one of the things that marks the Jazz listener. If you're listening to Jazz—if you're even thinking about listening to Jazz—you're already curious. However, one's curiosity need not be directionless, hence the creation of *The NPR Curious Listener's Guide to Jazz*, a book that will serve as a tour guide to both novice and seasoned Jazz listeners as they explore this richly diverse musical genre.

Indeed, Jazz music rewards a kind of restless, wide-ranging curiosity about life and the people and forces in it. There's a whole world—many worlds, in fact—waiting for you in Jazz music. It's proven itself to be endlessly adaptable to the cross-currents and often startling phenomena of modern life. Comedy, tragedy, high-mindedness, downhomeness, sophistication, pathos, joy—Jazz contains and celebrates all of these things and more. If you want to explore, if you're intellectually, emotionally, sensually, or socially inquisitive, then this music is out there waiting for you.

This book is here for you, too. It's a thorough guide to the music from a few basic perspectives: what it is and how it's made, its history, the people who made and continue to make it, some suggestions on how to approach it—and a whole pile of ideas. Jazz is a music not only of emotions and physical impulses, but also of ideas. The book's author, Loren Schoenberg, helps you explore these ideas and emotions. He knows Jazz as an accomplished musician, as a producer, as a scholar, and as one of its critical thinkers. You may not always agree with him, but that's part of Jazz, too: a lively exchange of thoughts within a strongly applied discipline.

Ours is a time when some of the most fundamental ways of life are being questioned. I think that makes our music more important than it's ever been because Jazz is an art form that depends on questioning, on challenging prevailing assumptions. Jazz music is an enjoyable, exhilarating, and expressive tool. It's a music that welcomes and entertains even as it investigates.

I've loved working with NPR over the years, especially on our "Jazz from Lincoln Center" series. I go around the country a lot, and it's safe to say there would almost be no Jazz on the air if it weren't for NPR and its member stations. I'm glad NPR is going beyond broadcasting, with efforts like their Jazz website, nprJazz.org, and *The NPR Curious Listener's Guide to Jazz*. I'm glad they got the right man for the job in Loren Schoenberg. And I'm glad that you're holding it in your hands right now. But most of all, I'm glad that we've found another Curious Listener, who's about to be a well-informed one, who is about to discover the delights, the wonders, the challenges, and the thrills waiting for you in our music—Jazz music, that is.

Introduction

Jazz is one of America's greatest contributions to the arts. Jazz is also a handy window into American history. But no one becomes a Jazz fan for those reasons. People become entranced with the music because of its rhythms and improvisatory nature. Jazz swings. When it doesn't swing, it is the exception rather than the rule. Jazz is fun. That does not mean it is only fun, or simply fun. What is it about a Jazz performance recorded in Chicago in the mid-1920s that proves irresistible to listeners halfway around the globe some three-quarters of a century later? At the root of Jazz is the act of playing: In a Jazz performance, and in the hands of true masters, the juggling act between the planned and the spontaneous creates a tension that makes each performance at once uniquely relevant to the moment of its creation and, if recorded, equally meaningful to subsequent generations. And it is this combination of elements that has enabled Jazz to be embraced as the favored mode of expression for countless peoples. Equally significant is the swinging optimism of the best Jazz, where the basic rhythm has a forward propulsion that strains at the edge of the beat, the swing element acting like a shot of adrenaline.

To be sure, there have been many other types of music in which improvisation played a role and in which the rhythmic momentum is a primary component of their appeal. But the specific combination of harmony, rhythm, and melody that defines Jazz has found a relevance in our culture—and other cultures—that these other types of music have not.

As Jazz enters its second century, and its original audience passes on, the appeal of its central figures remains secure. Watch a group of young people encountering classic Jazz for the first time, and this fact becomes abundantly clear. What is it about Louis Armstrong's "Black and Blue" that affects people so deeply? Or Fats Waller's "The Joint Is Jumpin'" that makes them smile? Why do even a few bars of Duke Ellington's theme song, "Take the 'A' Train," get at least some of their toes tapping? And how is it that they find the intensely spiritual and serious "A Love Supreme" by the John Coltrane Quartet so engrossing? It comes down to the timelessness of the art, and no matter how "dumbed down" or adolescent popular culture may have become in many respects, the sights and sounds of great artists engaging listeners' brains through their feet will always have a chance to communicate.

To those new ears, "New Orleans," "swing," "bop," "modal," "cool"—the established labels that have sown so much division within the Jazz world—mean nothing. Save for the difference in recording technology, the 1960 Ornette Coleman Quartet does not sound that far removed from the 1926 Jelly Roll Morton Red Hot Peppers. They are both making those quarter notes swing through both solo and group improvisation, and they are doing it in a musical manner steeped in the blues. In Jazz, as Albert Murray has noted, the blues is used as a medium of transcendence—one plays or sings the blues to vanquish them.

For many people, "serious" music is the kind you listen to while sitting in a concert hall, all dressed up, for long periods of time. Jazz evolved out of a world in which the music was a vital part of day-to-day existence. It was played at parties, in homes, on the street—anywhere and everywhere. And because it grew so quickly, from a folk art into a fine art within a matter of decades, the fact that a three-minute composition by someone named Jelly Roll Morton may tell us at least as much, if not more, about our culture than the much longer works of George Gershwin or Aaron Copland was hard to fathom, and still is in many quarters.

This book is intended to introduce readers unfamiliar with Jazz to this quintessentially contemporary music and to help make those already familiar with the music into better listeners. The major figures and their works will be explored, in part with an eye toward finding the common denominators that link their art and their lives with ours. The omission of all but a few Jazz vocalists is not intended as a slight and should not be taken as such. The emphasis in this short history will be on the definitive figures who have added significantly to the growing vocabulary of Jazz, and they are almost exclusively instrumentalists. Like all art forms, Jazz has its ever shifting canons, which are endlessly argued over. This is a good thing, for it speaks of an engagement and dialogue with the way that Jazz is understood in these rapidly changing times. To paraphrase one of Charlie Parker's classic blues, now is definitely the time to jump in and get your feet wet in the swirling world of music that is Jazz.

ONE

What Is Jazz?

What is Jazz? That's a question that has stymied the best and the brightest in the field since the music's inception. To some, it is defined by its distinctive musical profile, grounded in swinging 4/4 time with the blues as a touchstone. To others, its defining qualities are more abstract: a musical reflection of defiance or at least of antagonistic cooperation. Then there's the oft-cited definition supposedly uttered by an early Jazzman (usually said to be Louis Armstrong or Fats Waller): "If you have to ask, you'll never know"—which is enough to drive an inquisitive mind to despair.

This much, at least, can be said with relative confidence: Jazz is a music that first took shape in the cosmopolitan and musically sophisticated milieu of New Orleans in the early part of the twentieth century. It grew out of the many strands of vernacular American music that had found a home there—among them ragtime, originally a piano music that "ragged" the rhythms of popular (and relatively sophisticated) song styles, and blues, an essentially vocal music that laid plaintive stories over a simpler framework. Jazz drew, too, on other regional influences, including opera, which thrived in New Orleans in those years. Like blues and ragtime before it, Jazz was brought to life and nurtured by African-American musicians, and it remains at its core a fundamentally African-American idiom.

While the roots of Jazz are indelibly vocal, it evolved into primarily an instrumental genre, with its long series of innovations coming from instrumentalists. It is a music in which theme and variations play a large role, and in which each player has the potential role of composer. While it is not essential to know the tune a Jazz band is playing, it helps. In a Jazz band, the musical baton can be passed to any of its members and, as in a relay race, he or she takes responsibility for carrying the musical burden to the next signpost, where it can be handed over to someone else.

Jazz can be played on any instrument and by ensembles of any size. As a product of American culture, Jazz shares with that culture a protean quality that drives some to distraction and others to ecstasy. This has made Jazz a music that inspires a great passion and one that has yet to be satisfactorily defined, although there have been many brave attempts at it.

Perhaps the best way to arrive at a workable definition of Jazz is to use the music of Louis Armstrong as a benchmark. Armstrong's influence was, and remains, so seminal that relating any definition of Jazz must inevitably return to the work of this master trumpet player and vocalist. The essence of Armstrong's art was his willingness to use anything and everything available to him for artistic fodder and his resolve not to be constrained by what others considered to be clearly defined boundaries. And this is what the greatest Jazz musicians—like Duke Ellington, Charlie Parker, and John Coltrane—have continued to do: to look for vital inspiration across what to others have been uncrossable aesthetic borders.

What makes most Jazz music different from country, classical, rock, and the other well-known genres is its basic malleability. It is fair to generalize that when you hear a pop band or a symphony orchestra night after night, their performances of the same pieces remain more-or-less the same. Sure, there are subtle differences, but they are usually within the parameters of interpretation of a given text. With Jazz, we encounter something fundamentally different. The great majority of it is not, as many believe, spun out of the air, but is rather a highly organized and (hopefully) spontaneous set of theme and variations. And it is in the variations that the new and the dangerous can be conjured. This is what gives Jazz its special *frisson*. Even when Jazz is highly composed, as it is in most big bands, there can still be openings for improvisation that in the right hands can alter the context of the written sections so that no two performances are even similar.

It's essential to remember that the word *jazz* itself was problematic from the beginning. "Jass" evolved into "jazz" in the years surrounding World War I, and though its precise provenance has yet to be definitively resolved, it seems to have a clear link with sex and brothels and other things that aroused the interest of some and the condemnation of others.

Although few early Jazzmen in New Orleans actually played in brothels, the music has had great difficulty shaking its associations with the red-light district. (This may have more to do with the vestiges of racism in our society than it does with the music itself.) Jazz is usually said to have had "humble" origins, in that it was not conceived in the rarified precincts of "high" art; but in this regard it is no different from many other genres that have evolved into fine arts. But the word *jazz* had, and still has, negative connotations (e.g., "Don't give me any of that jazz"), which explains why as early as the 1920s some folks were already trying to disassociate themselves from the term *jazz*. Duke Ellington and others wanted to call what they wrote "American Negro music." But this effort came to naught, the word *jazz* stuck, and a lot of great music came of it.

In more strictly musical terms, Jazz is defined by its rhythmic qualities—the most essential one being "swing." Its melodies and harmonies came from Europe and were then filtered through the myriad strands that constituted the American experience. But its rhythmic profile was unique. The African component that survived through the years of slavery merged with the more evenly quantified nature of European rhythms to give Jazz its unique rhythmic lilt. Jazz is not alone in its resistance to being captured on the written music page.

There is a musical technique, familiar to classical pianists, known as rubato. One hand (usually the left) plays in strict tempo, while the other hand rushes and drags the beat, creating a tension that is resolved on a subsequent downbeat. In Jazz, the entire rhythm section in effect becomes the left hand, establishing and maintaining the beat, while the individual player becomes the adventurous right hand. Then there are rhythm-section players who themselves become the element of rhythmic counterpoint against the others. But what is it that makes the Jazz rubato different from its other variants? The catalytic nature of African culture is a given, and it was in the African-American church that this rhythmic elasticity was nurtured into the swinging rhythms that became indispensable elements of Jazz's creation.

Jazz's basic malleability allows it to embrace a range of styles as seemingly distinct as bop, swing, and fusion—and a range of musicians as individual as Sidney Bechet, Art Tatum, Dave Brubeck, and Wayne Shorter. And yet it is the central core of the music that allows all these styles and players to still remain incontestably Jazz. Therein lies the great wonder of Jazz, and its great strength.

TWO

The Story of Jazz

Any attempt to tell the story of as widely influential and improvisatory an art form as Jazz—and one that sprang up and came to maturity just as the recording industry was beginning to establish itself—would be a daunting challenge, no matter what the format. To do so in the span of a few dozen pages is next to impossible. Jazz evolved hand in glove with American culture, and that makes it especially difficult to pick and choose which strands to retain and which to eliminate. Still, there is much to be said for getting a sense of the big picture. Granted, the details might be a bit out of focus on occasion, but at least you have a starting point for appreciating exactly what happened and when, and then you can zero in on any of the thousands of details that captivate you.

The Roots of Jazz

Jazz is an essentially African-American musical phenomenon that evolved out of the unique historical, cultural, and social currents of eighteenth- and nineteenth-century New Orleans. The factors that underlie its emergence are many, but one stands above all: the fact that New Orleans was, at base, a French society. New Orleans had, after all, been the capital of French Louisiana since 1721, and although it was passed back and forth between France and Spain, by the time the U.S. took possession in 1803, a French outlook had taken firm root. To a remarkable degree, this held on despite the new American influences, and indeed still does today.

The French quality of New Orleans (as scholar Jerah Johnson has observed) was reflected most notably in a level of openness, tolerance, and freedom that simply could not be found in other (non-French) parts of the U.S. during the nation's formative years. This openness in large measure flowed from the economic agenda of the French colonial enterprise: They had come to the New World to make money and had simply found it smart business to welcome anyone who could help. The city became a destination for a wide range of outsiders—not just French, but Germans, Swiss, and other Europeans. Until the Civil War, slaveholding was widespread in New Orleans, but even in this respect the city was unique: Some slaves were free on weekends to participate in the city's work and social life, and they did. "Free" blacks also made New Orleans their home. The inclusive nature of New Orleans showed itself as well in the degree to which the various races intermingled and even intermarried—something all but unheard of in the English colonies and the states they would become. (None of this is to imply, of course, that the French experience in North America was without the complications, contradictions, and tragedies common to all colonialisms.)

The sense of tolerance in general, and the intermingling of the races in particular, also allowed for the development of a unique musical culture in New Orleans—a musical culture open to a great diversity of sounds and styles. Opera, for example, thrived in New Orleans, as did symphonic and chamber music. Caribbean music also made itself felt throughout the nineteenth century. The city's Congo Square served as a Sunday meeting place for slaves, and there the African musical legacy was given tangible expression. It is worth noting that even at this early stage, the interplay that would create Jazz was already at work since the folks in Congo Square couldn't help but reflect the music surrounding them.

With people of such distinct backgrounds commonly sharing social functions, music in New Orleans was obliged to appeal to many different ears. This quality was notably on display at the city's celebrated Quadroon Balls, among the most popular social events of the antebellum period. Here, a range of musical styles were mixed and matched, arranged and rearranged, all in an effort to keep the dancing guests satisfied. This ongoing quest for an inclusive, functional dance music would, in part, underlie the appearance of Jazz decades later.

The Birth of Jazz

The word *jazz* seems to have been born far away from New Orleans. It first shows up in sports columns written in

San Francisco in 1913, and it is clear that the term was already well ensconced in at least one segment of the population. It indicated the presence of a certain drive, enthusiasm, or "pep" in the lingo of the day, but within a short amount of time it also became ambiguous enough to have negative as well as positive connotations, as in "Don't give me any of that jazz." It is also clear that the term was not indigenous to New Orleans and that many of the early players from New Orleans first heard it after they had left home.

And in the same way that the genesis of the term remains nebulous, so does the music's provenance. We do know what led up to it—ragtime and the blues, the brass bands that played in New Orleans, and the many other formations that were popular at the turn of the century. Ragtime was at its inception an African-American music that transformed the popular piano music of the day through a bracing syncopation that seemed to "rag" the notes into different shapes. These shapes were born of the dance steps that flourished in the black communities. The blues, based on a simple yet elegant three-chord construction, had originated in the vocal expressions of slaves in the Deep South. They found their way into the popular vernacular through the pioneering work of W. C. Handy, and by the mid-teens, the blues had gained widespread popularity in New Orleans and elsewhere. The brass bands spawned a group of horn players who learned to extemporize in a ragtime fashion, and in keeping with New Orleans' tendency toward the crossing of musical styles, they began to blend it with the other styles that were current, including blues.

The precise juncture at which music made that fateful turn from a raggy sort of brass-band sound into the idiom that spawned Louis Armstrong has been lost to history. We do know many of the contributing factors (including string bands), and recent research has been shedding much-needed light on an area shrouded in myth. The consensus remains that cornetist Buddy Bolden, whose band peaked around 1905 (just a year before he was committed to an insane asylum), brought a blues-edged dynamism to his playing that captivated anyone who heard it. On the other hand, guitarist Johnny St. Cyr recalled hearing The Golden Rule Band doing much the same thing around much the same time as Bolden, only better. It is just one more piece of evidence that there was a general movement under way at the time that was nudging this genre toward a newfound balance of improvisation, melodic paraphrase, and composition that was unique in Western music.

Throughout the 1910s, musicians such as pianist Jelly Roll Morton and cornetist King Oliver (and many, many others) were establishing themselves as primary exponents of this new New Orleans music. It was still not called "Jazz" in its birthplace, but it was beginning to take on its signature characteristics. The lack of recordings during this seminal period is frustrating, but the fully mature recordings these New Orleans musicians made in the next decade suggest that the great bulk of the transition from blues and ragtime to Jazz occurred in the mid-teens.

Enter Louis Armstrong

Although he didn't become a great figure in popular entertainment until the early '30s, Armstrong sent off enough

Bolden Out Loud

Buddy Bolden was said to have played so forcefully that his trumpet could be heard all over New Orleans. Given the fact that there is little documentation of the man himself, much less his music, this was thought to be just another Crescent City myth. But was it? New Orleans, after all, lies below sea level, and it has acoustical properties like those of an echo chamber. Add to that the lack of cars and similar distractions at that time, and maybe the stories about Bolden sticking his cornet out of a club to alert the town to his presence really are true.

sparks throughout the '20s to energize an entire generation of musicians. He took the best of the elegant tradition of New Orleans brass men who had preceded him (among them King Oliver, Freddie Keppard, Mutt Carey, Bunk Johnson) and created something so human and so beautiful that it was only a matter of time until the world caught on. In fact, one might use Armstrong's career as a common denominator for considering all of the subsequent directions Jazz took, for the musical threads Armstrong spun during his fifty-year career are still a vital part of Jazz fabric even into the twenty-first century. This should come as no surprise given his essential role in defining the music as a fine art.

What Armstrong did, in essence, was merge the language and the improvisatory essence of the blues with whatever music he encountered. Whether it was excerpts from opera, symphonic or chamber music, ragtime—you name it—

Armstrong was able to play the blues over it. To be sure, he was in turn profoundly influenced by opera in general, due to its great popularity in New Orleans—and specifically by the recordings of the tenor Enrico Caruso—and by the sophisticated harmonies and melodies that were vital parts of the music that swirled around New Orleans. The magic happened when Armstrong took all of the influences into what was undeniably an African-American idiom and made a new whole out of what remained in other, lesser hands, component segments. But it was the transformative essence of his music that defined what Jazz was to become—an African-American idiom in which anyone, from anywhere, could make vital contributions.

Armstrong emerged into the mainstream of the New Orleans musical establishment as a disciple of King Oliver. Until his dying day, he would always credit Oliver as his most important influence; but like many other great geniuses, he had no compunction about taking anything he could use from any source. It was his good fortune to come of musical age in New Orleans, a city overflowing with musical vitality. Indeed, when Oliver left town in 1919, Armstrong, though still only a teenager, joined Kid Ory's band, which was widely regarded as one of the best. An extended engagement with Fate Marable's band (which played on a riverboat that went up and down the Mississippi) followed, and it was here that Armstrong honed his reading and ensemble skills. Though he had received offers to leave New Orleans from such prominent New York musicians as Fletcher Henderson, Armstrong was content to stay in his hometown and provide for his family. It wasn't until Oliver beckoned for him to come to Chicago in late 1922 that Armstrong finally left, and just a few months later made his first recordings on Oliver's own first record date. It was the exposure that he gained as a member of Oliver's band that led Henderson to offer him a second chance at New York, and with the urging of his wife, pianist Lil Hardin, he accepted the challenge in late 1924.

Armstrong represented the coming together of all of the various strands of New Orleans music that had been gestating over the previous decade. His style was so perfect and so relevant that it quickly became Jazz's lingua franca. No less a figure than Duke Ellington characterized Armstrong's arrival in Fletcher Henderson's band in 1924 New York this way: ". . . nobody had ever heard anything like it, and his impact cannot be put in words."

Jazz Leaves Home

The changes that Jazz went through between the years 1917–1929 were remarkable. It began to branch out from its New Orleans roots, with many of its pioneers spreading the message directly—Oliver and Armstrong in Chicago, for example. It was during the First World War that the famed red-light district of New Orleans, known as "Storyville," was closed by the government for a variety of reasons, purportedly including the fact that too many servicemen were going AWOL there during their transfers in New Orleans. But the upshot of the closing was that the large musical community that had found bountiful work there for years suddenly had to reestablish itself elsewhere.

This was part of the Great Migration that was moving a

Lincoln and Armstrong

Gary Wills, in his masterful *Lincoln at Gettysburg*, makes the case that Lincoln redefined our system of government with that one short speech. This story finds an instructive parallel in Armstrong's streamlining of New Orleans polyphony, melodic paraphrase, the grand gesture of opera, and, of course, the blues, into a musical discipline that merged improvisation and composition in a new way. Both Lincoln and Armstrong were able to make profound statements in an extraordinarily concise manner, while at the same time subtly redefining the basic principles of their given texts: in Lincoln's case, the Constitution, in Armstrong's, American music.

During his lifetime, Lincoln did not enjoy the reverence he now commands. His combination of folktales, analogies, and humor resulted in his being dismissed and insulted in some quarters as a buffoon incapable of appreciating the seriousness of high, democratic politics. Because Armstrong had so many layers of Americana in his personality—from hard street smarts to verbal slapstick to extraordinary musical elegance—he often has been seen as someone who could not have actually possessed the musical intelligence that he so consistently exhibited. Like those who thought of Lincoln as a country boy with feet too small for the shoes of the presidency, there are still those who define Armstrong as no more than a noble savage. Jazz music, in all of its current glory, renders the most eloquent refutation of that solecism.

large segment of the South's population up North. The change of America's economy from rural to industrial, and a desire by African Americans to escape the overriding racism of the

South, spawned large black populations in Northern cities such as Chicago. Naturally, the musicians followed, and the subsequent mixture of the music's New Orleans roots with the more urban styles of the Northern cities accelerated Jazz's evolution.

Sidney Bechet, master of both the clarinet and the soprano saxophone, toured Europe with Will Marion Cook's Syncopated Southern Orchestra in 1919 to great acclaim. European audiences were already well acclimated to African-American music, having given a warm reception to the Fisk Jubilee singers (whose renditions of Negro spirituals were a precursor of gospel music) in the late 1870s, and later having embraced ragtime. Back on the home front, where such profound recognition was still a long time coming, many of the most significant New Orleans Jazz greats eventually settled in Chicago (after trips to other areas, including California), and by the mid-twenties, King Oliver and Jelly Roll Morton and their bands were in great demand. Besides their busy engagement schedules, they were making the recordings that defined the basis of Jazz. The Creole Jazz Band and the Red Hot Peppers opened the window on the glory of New Orleans polyphony as it evolved from the teens through the twenties.

During this same time period, vocal blues almost took over the recording industry. Spurred by Mamie Smith's 1920s recording of "Crazy Blues," all of the labels scurried to sign up African-American women who could sing the blues. In a wonderful merging of popular taste and true artistry, the great Bessie Smith began a series of recordings in 1923 that both sold well and documented the tremendous sophistication that dwelled in what some at the time (both black and white) thought of, if they thought of it at all, as the devil's music. Ethel Waters, while herself a superlative blues singer, ranged further in her stylistic boundaries than did Bessie Smith. Her superb diction and subtle, rhythmic sense helped her cover a wide repertoire that eventually made her a favorite of both black and white audiences.

But the presence of all of this wonderful Jazz and Jazz-related blues music on the air, in the clubs and theaters, and on recordings did more in the end to establish African Americans themselves instead of the reductive and distorted imagery of minstrelsy as an essential component of American culture than did the more self-conscious efforts of the Harlem Renaissance.

Jazz was also disseminated through recordings and, to a lesser extent, the new medium of radio. It established itself as a vital part of the musical marketplace with the advent of the Original Dixieland Jazz Band recordings of 1917. Though theirs was a pale reflection of the breadth and depth of New Orleans Jazz, without their huge commercial breakthrough the subsequent "Jazz Age" may (as Albert Murray has noted) have had a noticeably different musical profile. From this point on, the importance of recordings in both the development of the music itself and in its ability to be listened to outside of the context of dance music cannot be overstated. It allowed repeated listening to music that was largely improvised, and permitted a generation of musicians to use these recordings in the same way that previous generations had used the printed score.

And since Jazz was a part of the burgeoning popular-music world, Jazz bands began to pop up all over the world. The great majority of these were novelty bands, offering not much more than a reflection of Jazz's superficial elements, but Jazz was also taking on a new dimension as high art. For the first time, it was becoming apparent that Jazz was at once a popular music, a functional (dance) music, and an art form on a par with any other—and perhaps the most significant cultural contribution born in the United States. As the early '20s progressed, a handful of bands emerged that not only took the music seriously, but had new things to offer. A significant aspect of this was that a whole generation of young, white musicians were eagerly dedicating their lives to a pursuit in which the acknowledged masters were African American. This would have a significant effect on the popular culture of the following decade when one of them, Benny Goodman, surprisingly morphed from an excellent Jazz clarinetist who played commercial music for a living into a cultural icon. The decisions he made once he attained that status were also to be of great import.

Jazz Through the 1920s

In a sense, the story of Jazz revolves around musicians becoming their own Louis Armstrongs, with the innovators being the ones who inject the greatest proportions of their own individuality into it. Indeed, in coming to terms with Jazz, the terms *reconciliation* and *innovation* need to be pushed closer together than they usually are, as the first major solo voice to emerge after Armstrong demonstrates.

The cornetist Bix Beiderbecke was at once entranced by the artistry of Armstrong and the singers Ethel Waters and

High Praise for Bechet

The Swiss conductor Ernest Ansermet, known for his work with Igor Stravinsky, heard Bechet play in 1919, which inspired him to write a lengthy review. He wrote, in part: "The first thing that strikes one about the Southern Syncopated Orchestra is the astonishing perfection, the superb taste, and the fervor of the playing . . . There is . . . an extraordinary virtuoso who is, it seems, the first of his race to have composed perfectly formed blues on the clarinet. I've heard two of them which he had elaborated at great length, then played to his companions so that they were equally admirable for their richness of invention, force of accent, and daring in novelty and the unexpected. Already, they have given the idea of a style, and their form was gripping, abrupt, harsh, with a brusque and pitiless ending like that of Bach's Brandenburg Concerto. I wish to set down the name of this artist of genius; as for myself, I shall never forget it—it is Sidney Bechet."

Bessie Smith while also steeped in the safely experimental harmonies of such composers of light classics as Americans Eastwood Lane and Edward MacDowell. He managed to bring these seeming opposites together in his introverted style. The improvisation and blues tonality place it squarely within the African-American oeuvre, and Bix (along with his musical partner, the saxophonist Frank Trumbauer) placed a different emphasis on certain parts of the musical scale than anyone else did at the time. This resulted in solos that abounded in melodic shapes new to Jazz and that were to have forceful consequences within a decade's time. Their conception, through their solos and their influence on the band's arrangers (most notably Bill Challis), profoundly affected the way that Paul Whiteman's band played in the late '20s.

Whiteman was, literally and figuratively, one of the biggest men in the popular-music field in the '20s, and the fact that he gave a lot of exposure to Beiderbecke and Trumbauer meant that their music was heard by millions. The great majority of those listeners would never have had the opportunity to come across an Oliver, Morton, or an early Armstrong record. Saxophonist Lester Young was just one of the musicians who heard these records and who found something that he could use in his own quest to be a Jazz individual. And besides the musicians, a public began to emerge for the more artistic Jazz recordings.

Meanwhile, Armstrong himself returned to Chicago in 1925 and besides playing in big bands and theater orchestras, recorded the famous Hot Fives and Sevens. These small-group recordings established the Jazz vocabulary that the music is still reacting to, and they also established Armstrong as a leader in his own right. After years of towering over his colleagues, Armstrong finally had recorded with someone with whom he could thrust and parry—pianist Earl Hines. Their 1928 recordings were among the most significant of the era. Armstrong was no longer limited to brilliant soliloquies, but was now able to engage in coherent musical dialogues with someone else.

Armstrong went back to New York in 1929, and within a few years' time had conquered Broadway, movies, radio, and film. The significance of his ascension to world fame cannot be overstated. We have been living in his musical world for so long now that it is difficult to realize how much a part of our contemporary culture his innovations remain.

Armstrong waded into a popular culture where young, white Americans danced to "The Charleston," composed by James P. Johnson. It created a furor in 1923 and is still the dance most readily associated with the Jazz Age. It was the specific syncopation of the music, in this case anticipating the downbeats, that made the dance as visually provocative as the music itself was. What separated Johnson from the great majority of his peers was his desire to combine not only ragtime and the European classics, but also to incorporate the "shout" dances he had witnessed as a child. At that time, (and to some degree, to this day), virtually every African-American community, no matter its location, had a direct link to its Southern heritage. Johnson heard native Virginians sing and dance in his New Jersey church in a way that made an indelible impression on him. The result was a rhythmic dynamism that later became known as "swing" and was the edifice on which Louis Armstrong built his radical transformations. It was also further proof to the public at large that much of popular entertainment came directly from black Americans.

Johnson was the prime figure in the advent of a style of piano playing that evolved in and around New York in the '20s known as "stride." The name came from the expert left-hand figures that alternated between lower single or octave notes and higher, more fully fingered chords. To master it, one had to be able to play in any key and produce a seemingly unending series of spontaneous variations on a wide variety of themes. The main creators include James P. Johnson and Willie "The Lion" Smith. Among their disciples were Fats Waller, Duke Ellington, and Count Basie, each of whom branched off on his own and created his own school of influence.

The Big Bands

Throughout the 1920s, big bands were becoming the ensemble of choice for popular dance music. Indeed, Jazz found its ultimate voice in the big band, which is to American culture what the symphony orchestra is for Europeans. The classic instrumentation of trumpets, trombones, saxophone, and a rhythm section evolved out of the dance bands of the late teens and early twenties. Among the most important figures in this genesis were the bandleader Art Hickman and his arranger Ferde Grofé, who heard New Orleans Jazzmen playing in San Francisco in the early 1910s and set out to capture their essence in his orchestrations for Hickman's band. Their use of a saxophone section and the interplay between the different groups of instruments helped to create a matrix for what became big band Jazz in the '20s.

There were many wonderful big bands from the mid-twenties through the late '40s, but there are a handful that predominate. By virtue of their soloists and/or the composers and arrangers they hired, these bands rose to the top in what was an extraordinarily competitive market, for this was the music that appealed to the country's youth. In terms of Jazz, one has to start with Fletcher Henderson's band. It was a hotbed of Jazz activity, with arranger Don Redman and tenor

The Lion

There was quite a bit of interaction between the stride-piano giants and the Tin Pan Alley and Broadway composers of the '20s. You can hear it in the music. Willie "The Lion" Smith was known to be fiercely proud of his piano virtuosity and once said of the legendary "cutting" contests where fellow pianists would gather to try and top one another: "We would embroider the melodies with our own original ideas and try to develop patterns that had more originality than those played before us. Sometimes it was just a question of who could think up the most patterns within a given tune. It was pure improvisation." One of his most legendary moments came one night at a party when the young George Gershwin tried to get something going at the piano. No sooner had he gotten started when the Lion barked in his inimitable fashion: "Get up off that piano bench, you tomato!" and proceeded to give him a lesson.

saxophonist Coleman Hawkins in 1924–25 picking up quickly on what their band mate Louis Armstrong was doing. By using Armstrong's innovations as a springboard for their own creativity, they gave the Jazz world at large a blueprint for individuality.

The group that laid the groundwork for the ensuing commercial explosion of swing was the Casa Loma Band, from Canada. Their combination of high energy (more "peppy" than swinging, but engaging nonetheless), fantastic articulation, and imaginative arrangements made them a favorite at colleges around the country during the early '30s, and they helped to create the audience for Benny Goodman and the other bands that followed in his wake. This is not to say that there weren't other bands with stronger Jazz credentials, but that is not what makes for a shift in musical culture. It is a matter of being in the right place at the right time doing the right thing, and Casa Loma fit the bill by offering the masses of white youth a new sound that was different from what they were hearing elsewhere.

The fact that the roots of the music were indelibly African American was at first played down by the media. It remained for Goodman, once his band started the swing ball rolling in the summer of 1935, to publicly credit Fletcher Henderson and the other black arrangers who were at the root of his success. But Goodman also added something of his own to the musical mix, and in the process, integrated his band with pianist Teddy Wilson and vibraphonist Lionel Hampton. He was also, along with his future brother-in-law John Hammond, responsible for bringing the Count Basie band out of Kansas City.

The playing field was far from even between the white and black bands of the Swing Era, but it was a time when the first efforts were made at presenting to the public the truth about where the music actually came from. What could not be denied was the extraordinary volume of great art that poured out of these bands. Jimmie Lunceford, Basie, Ellington, Goodman, Chick Webb, Artie Shaw, Cab Calloway, Glenn Miller, Claude Thornhill, and Tommy Dorsey all led bands that were tremendously successful from a business perspective and which also made great music with varying degrees of commercialism, each with its own style.

There were also many bands known as "territory bands" that were strongly based in their local provinces, though they did travel. Some of them recorded, leaving behind wonderful documents of a time when there were still regional sounds around the country.

The Swing Era

In the face of a great economic depression and the eventual outbreak of the Second World War, American popular-musical culture hit a high-water mark in which stylistic elegance and sophistication were rewarded with mass acceptance. This is not to say that the era was anymore free of trash than any other, it's just that the lowest common denominator was much higher than it was before, or has been since. The big band was the quintessential Swing Era unit, and as such bears some examination.

There is an intersection between composition and improvisation that depends on the soloist's ability to create within the construct designed by the composer/arranger. In other words, there is a frame within which the soloist must operate. The more he or she can relate to what came before, what is coming, and what is happening in the background, the better the solo will be. And he must do this by using his own creativity and speaking in his own musical voice, with the natural adjustments made for the specific context.

Various sections of a composition can be reordered, extended, shortened, or elaborated as the moment dictates. This is why many consider the big band the ultimate ensemble for Jazz. At the drop of a hat, it can be reconstituted from a solo instrument into any number of a dozen different configurations, undergirded by the innate strength of the composition at hand.

In many ways, this is the period when the seeds that Armstrong had planted in the '20s bore fruit. His phrasing was adapted by both individual players and by entire bands. Jazz composers/arrangers developed their own variations on his language, and his radical redefinition of how to sing a popular song became a major influence on the new generation of popular singers. Almost every band had someone who sang or played in a style that was in direct homage to Armstrong.

There were dozens of first-rate big-band soloists who mastered the swing style (and used Armstrong's style as a springboard for their own creativity). A choice list would include: the trumpeters Roy Eldridge and Frankie Newton; the trombonists Jack Jenney and Dicky Wells; the reedmen Lester Young and Johnny Hodges; the pianists Jess Stacy and Billy Kyle; the guitarist Charlie Christian; the bassist Jimmy Blanton; and the drummers Chick Webb, Sid Catlett, and Ray McKinley—as well as the ever-experimental Red Norvo, who played the xylophone, marimba, and vibraphone.

The Swing Era began in the depths of the Depression and ended along with the conclusion of World War II in 1945, when tastes changed. Postwar youth wanted something of their own, leading to another seismic shift in mass taste. It took awhile for this to trickle down, and there remained many vestiges of the Swing Era throughout the early '50s, but the sense of urgency and innovation was gone. Singers, small groups, and eventually rock and roll were the primary agents heralding this change—as was the economic reality of maintaining a big band, which had become prohibitively expensive.

Beyond the Big Bands

The big bands did not have a monopoly on good Jazz during the Swing Era. There were many small groups that stood out for their originality and quality. The John Kirby Sextet was the first black band to have a network radio show, and they possessed a rare combination of virtuosity (which hovered near the surface of most of their music, yet it was never off-putting), good taste, and musical humor. There was the Nat Cole Trio that set the standard for piano, guitar, and bass combinations. No pianist was more famous than Thomas "Fats" Waller, who led a septet known as his "rhythm," and although his mugging and general demeanor were used to comic ends, his playing was never anything less than immaculate.

One of the most outstanding Jazz artists of all time who established himself as an attraction during the Swing Era was pianist Art Tatum. He delivered a virtuosic style that reached new and as yet unsurpassed levels of technical and harmonic/rhythmic sophistication. His influence transcended the piano. Saxophonist Coleman Hawkins, for instance, was profoundly affected by the harmonic freedom with which Tatum played. And it was the fleet-fingered Hawkins who inspired the young

Goodman at Carnegie and Savoy

Ask any swing fan to tell you which day he would return to if he had a time machine, and the answer for many would be January 16, 1938. That was the evening of Benny Goodman's legendary Carnegie Hall Concert. There had been Jazz played there before, to be sure, but this was a cultural event that put the music squarely on the concert map. Goodman's band was in peak form (Harry James, Lionel Hampton, Teddy Wilson, and Gene Krupa), and the leader had invited guests from the Ellington and Basie bands to sit in as featured soloists. The concert was recorded privately and given to Goodman as a memento. He stored the discs away, and when they were uncovered twelve years later stashed in a closet, Goodman had dubs made, which led to a commercial release. It has remained one of the best-selling Jazz albums of all time. So far, so good. But the music that followed the concert that night, up at Harlem's Savoy Ballroom, was at least as thrilling as the Goodman concert.

Count Basie's band (with Billie Holiday and Lester Young) was just establishing itself in the first rank of swing bands, having only arrived from Kansas City a year earlier. They were placed right in the lion's den that night in a battle with the Savoy's favorite band, led by drummer Chick Webb and featuring vocalist Ella Fitzgerald. The Goodman band and any and all swing aficionados went directly to the Savoy from Carnegie and witnessed a battle of the bands that still has the surviving witnesses disputing who won. Ellington himself was persuaded to play a number, and, according to a contemporary review, "sounded so good that Basie's band picked it up and swung right along with him," producing "a highlight of the evening."

Roy Eldridge to develop a multinoted way of playing trumpet solos that was dramatically different from Armstrong's more declamatory utterances.

It was also during this period that the first great female Jazz vocalists appeared. Both were steeped in Armstrong, but used it to different ends. Billie Holiday made something original out of Armstrong's more abstract phrasing and blues essence (she was also a Bessie Smith fan), while Ella Fitzgerald was equally impressed with the smoother stylings of pop singers such as Connie Boswell, and sounded far more conventional.

Armstrong himself continued to develop through this period, playing with more space and paring things down to the essentials. Two of his star sidemen, Lionel Hampton and Teddy Wilson, listened carefully to the more subtle aspects of his playing and emerged as important stylists in their own right. When they became members of the Benny Goodman small groups in the mid-thirties, a blow was struck for racial integration. And on a musical level, they pioneered a new kind of chamber Jazz that was founded in a tremendous virtuosity and an equally high level of swing. Thanks to the high profile the Goodman gig afforded them, they undertook an extended series of recording sessions featuring all-star bands, resulting in some of the most important recordings of the era.

All of this was occurring as America's popular culture approached its zenith in the years surrounding World War II. While there were pockets of serious listeners around the world, including some of the very first publications to take the music seriously, for most it remained a functional dance music. One of the main reasons for its popularity in encouraging what Ellington liked to refer to as the "terpsichorean urge" was the buoyancy of Jazz rhythm.

Bird, Diz, and Bop

By the end of the '30s, a new generation of players had appeared who felt stifled by the ubiquity of big bands and their limited opportunities for full-blown improvisation. Some of the best of them gathered in a handful of after-hours clubs in Harlem. All were musical descendants of Armstrong who were acknowledging their own influences and gradually finding their own voices. They included the electric guitarist Charlie Christian, the trumpeter Dizzy Gillespie, the drummer Kenny Clarke, the pianist Thelonious Monk, and the bassist Jimmy Blanton (heard in the great 1939–41 Ellington band). These young lions also listened closely to Blanton's band mates, saxophonist Ben Webster and composer Billy Strayhorn. They began to devise challenging material to discourage lesser talents from jamming with them, and found that they liked what they came up with enough to pursue it on its own terms. An infrequent but vital presence was saxophonist Charlie Parker, who, like Lester Young, was on the verge of becoming almost as influential a figure as Armstrong. And also like Young, Parker brought together the seemingly conflicting musical philosophies that to the great majority of his peers were mutually exclusive. Parker adapted large chunks of both what Lester Young and Coleman Hawkins (mostly through his disciple Ben Webster) represented, and made them his own.

Swing and Dance

Musicians who first play classic, big-band music in nondance settings are often amazed when they first see dancers move to the music. Many of the rhythmic figures, melodic shapes, and even aspects of the orchestration are only fully revealed when danced to. Dancing is basically a narrative function—it tells a story. Music also tells a story, but in a more abstract form, and the merging of the two disciplines only amplifies the opportunities for personal interpretation. It is also possible to imagine when not dancing how the movement to a particular piece might go, and this can be a healthy solution for dealing with that urge when it would be inappropriate to just jump up and let go. As the great Jazz writer Albert Murray put it in his invaluable *Stompin' the Blues*, ". . . dance, according to impressive anthropological data, seems to have been the first means by which human consciousness objectified, symbolized, and stylized its perceptions, conceptions and feelings. Thus the very evidence that suggests that the pragmatic function of concert music is to represent the dancing attitudes also serves to reinforce the notion that dance is indispensable." And then there is always the option of getting hold of a recording of a favorite piece and cutting a carpet at home. Ellington knew all about this; in his written introduction to "Harlem Air Shaft," he noted that the jitterbugs always lived above you, never below!

After playing together in the bands of Earl Hines and Billy Eckstine, Charlie Parker and Dizzy Gillespie formed their own quintet in 1945. They played on 52nd Street in midtown

Manhattan, which since the mid-thirties had been home to a phalanx of clubs that housed bands (mostly combos) that played for listening only. As a team they were formidable. Gillespie had the organizational skills both for performing and for business that allowed them to present their own music on their own terms. He was also one of Jazz's great teachers. He instructed musicians of every instrument how to play the new music. It was a style that reveled in super-fast tempos, dissonant harmonies, and a challenging melodic angularity. Parker supplied the pure, unadulterated genius that brought it all to a new level. Like Armstrong, he was able to "play the blues" on top of anything, no matter how complex the context, and it was this ability that gave his work its great accessibility.

This new music was given the name "bebop" (also called "rebop" in its early years, but nowadays almost always reduced to the more utilitarian "bop"). It was purely onomatopoeic, being nothing more than Gillespie's attempt to sing one of its characteristic rhythms to a Jazz writer, who then used it mercilessly to create and christen a new fad.

A recording ban begun by the musicians union in August 1942 (in protest to radio stations' playing of recordings instead of employing live musicians) had largely kept the newly emerging sound under wraps. So when the first recordings of Parker and Gillespie came out in the spring of 1945, they were doubly shocking. All of this was occurring at the same time that the Big Band Era was drawing to a close due to changing tastes in popular music and shifts in the way the entertainment business was taxed. Small groups and singers replaced the big bands, and it only seemed natural that the "modern" Jazz combos would take their place. But it was the Bebopers' fate to be caught on the side of greater sophistication in music at a time when American culture was heading firmly in the direction that led to the advent of Elvis Presley in 1954.

Gillespie and Parker parted as co-leaders in early 1946. Both of their subsequent bands were to be essential training grounds for the best of the next generation. Miles Davis, who played trumpet in Parker's quintet, was at first thought to be an odd choice since he had none of the flash and virtuosity that distinguished Gillespie. But that was what made him such a perfect contrast to Parker's brilliance. By the time he began making his own recordings as a leader, it was clear that Davis was an original thinker who had a complementary, but quite different concept than Parker did about how the music should go.

Davis realized that the simple formula of melody-solos-melody could get stale rather fast, so he forged a fresh approach. He worked with a number of composer/arrangers, most notably Gil Evans, to blend composition and improvisation in the way that Ellington had, but with the tone colors of the great Claude Thornhill Orchestra, which used woodwinds, French horns, and tuba. This was in later years referred to as the "Birth of the Cool" band. The band failed commercially, and Davis eventually formed a series of small groups in which his increasingly spare and thoughtful phrasing made for a wonderful contrast with the more multinoted improvisations of saxophonists Sonny Rollins and John Coltrane.

Diz at Carnegie

Gillespie's band played its first Carnegie Hall concert on September 29, 1947. The hall was sold out, and like the Goodman concert almost a decade earlier, it was a watershed for a "new" music's cultural and commercial ascendancy. Gillespie's band played their most demanding works, including the premiere of pianist John Lewis's ambitious composition "Toccata for Trumpet." Ella Fitzgerald also did a set with the band, but the pièce de résistance was a reunion of Gillespie and Charlie Parker. They revived the classic repertoire with which they had started the whole bop thing a few years earlier on 52nd Street. Parker was so moved that, according to Dizzy, "[he] just walked out on the stage with one rose, one long rose—he'd probably spent his last quarter to buy it—and gave it to me. And he kissed me—on the mouth—and then walked off. I get a warm feeling every time I think about Charlie Parker." The recordings of the evening reveal both men in absolutely top form. What we are hearing is not only a glorious redefinition of the potential of musical instruments, but one of the two most vital contributions ever made to the Jazz language. When Parker played these solos, he may very well have looked into the audience and there met the eyes of Louis Armstrong, the only other American in whom the past, the present, and the future of Jazz continued to reside.

Other Musicians, Other Sounds

The other major innovator of the late '40s was the pianist Lennie Tristano. He schooled his disciples, which included saxophonists Lee Konitz and Warne Marsh, in the music of Young, Eldridge, and Armstrong, but the result sounded radically different. Tristano's goal was to even the music out rhythmically while pushing its harmonic and melodic boundaries. To some, this distorted the natural tension between harmony, rhythm, and melody and gave the music an academic feeling. To others, he was a musical prophet. One avenue he explored before anyone else was "free" improvisation with no preset chord structure or time signature.

It was during the late '40s that the novelty of bop wore off. It was becoming apparent to many of the musicians involved that while it was a perfect mode of expression for players of Parker and Gillespie's brilliance, in lesser hands it was quickly degenerating into a morass of immature clichés. Miles Davis addressed this by reinstating a strong compositional element that drew heavily on the best of the Big Band Era with his nonet. There were others, such as the pianist/composers Tadd Dameron, Dave Brubeck, and George Russell, who asserted their own voices at this time. Their work is hard to fit into any of the usual stylistic categories. Nonetheless, the name given much of the new music of this period was "cool." In the early 1950s, a group of white players (many of whom were from the East Coast) established themselves in and around Los Angeles, where there was bountiful work in the still largely segregated film and recording studios. Their version of cool Jazz became known as West Coast Jazz. It was in response to the perceived distortion of some of Jazz's most basic elements in this music that a group of black musicians on the East Coast began calling their music, with its inspiration in gospel music and the blues, hard bop. At fifty years removed, it can safely be said that neither West Coast Jazz nor hard bop were free of cliché or of a subsequent hardening of the aesthetic arteries. But the social climate they grew out of remains a significant factor when assessing their historic context.

As the '50s progressed, the preeminence of tenor saxophonist Sonny Rollins became more pronounced. Unlike the great majority of his peers, he felt no need to jettison all of the expressive and musical devices of the music's past to express his thoroughly contemporary ruminations. Indeed, the broader his frame of reference became (by the late '50s, he improvised in a fashion that frequently brought Louis Armstrong to mind), the further into the future he probed. And although he was a few years younger than John Coltrane, Rollins was the man to beat as the decade drew to a close.

Jazz still had enough of a commercial profile in the '50s to sustain a large number of working bands. Among the most significant were:

▪ The Modern Jazz Quartet, whose musical director, pianist John Lewis, used a wide array of compositional devices to organize his music to unfold more organically than the standard patterns that were rapidly becoming the norm in almost all Jazz groups.

▪ Art Blakey's Jazz Messengers, led by a dynamic drummer who consistently hired the best young players and featured their music with an emphasis on a group sound with lots of ensemble work.

▪ Miles Davis's Quintet and Sextet, which by the mid-fifties had become the definitive influence in small group Jazz. Davis had a disdain for cliché, and as soon as he felt his band's work had become the slightest bit stale, he would make a change.

- Charles Mingus's various groups, which ranged from small combos to large ensembles. Like John Lewis, Mingus saw no reason to jettison the formal parts of the Jazz tradition that created contrast in performance. Unlike Lewis, Mingus was a relentless provocateur who reveled in making his bands and his audiences uncomfortable if he felt the slightest twinge of complacency on their parts.

- The Dave Brubeck Quartet was tremendously popular and served as an introduction to "modern" Jazz for a generation of young people who otherwise might never have found it. Their repertoire was varied and challenging, and their hit recording of "Take Five" (in the challenging meter of 5/4) achieved iconic status.

- Gerry Mulligan's small bands were notable for their omission of a piano. A master of counterpoint both as a writer and as an improviser, Mulligan set himself against a smoothly swinging rhythm section and first-rate, frontline partners to create music of a delicate and intellectual nature.

This was also the time period when Thelonious Monk gradually attained his due as one of the preeminent player/composers in Jazz. Though his public profile played up the eccentric nature of his personality, it was the inevitability and depth of his music that eventually established his reputation. During the late '50s, Monk, along with Davis and Rollins, achieved a structural unity in their playing that was a rare and miraculous occurrence. The earliest and the most contemporary conventions were audible and at the same time, a new generation, including Wayne Shorter, Andrew Hill, Herbie Hancock, and Chick Corea, was finding inspiration in his work for the new sounds that would occur in the '60s and that form the basis for much of today's Jazz.

The '50s also saw the emergence of what became known as "third-stream music," which eventually proved to be a dead end, but which produced some very interesting results during its decade of prominence. The musicians active in this effort (led by Gunther Schuller) were picking up on a tendency that the bandleader Stan Kenton had started in the late '40s with his attempts to "innovate," most of which had been too self-conscious and of little import. But the works of Bill Russo and Bob Graettinger did break some significant ground in Jazz composition, and when Bill Holman, Gerry Mulligan, Lee Konitz, and Mel Lewis were in various editions of Kenton's bands in the mid-fifties, they actually swung!

Probably the greatest band of the era to regularly explore unusual instrumentations and unorthodox techniques was the Sauter-Finegan Orchestra. Led by two of the most idiosyncratic composer/arrangers of the Swing Era, they had an accidental hit with "The Doodletown Fifers" in 1952, and kept the band together for the rest of the decade. Though their recordings are hard to find, it is well worth the trouble, for their sense of experimentation and intelligence was matched by a sense of humor and healthy dose of self-deprecation that Kenton and the other contemporary bandleaders, who tried all sorts of "modern" experiments, could dearly have used.

Pushing the Boundaries

"Free Jazz" represented a much sharper break with the conventions inherent in all previous styles; in other words, the idea that an improvisation need not be based on any chord structure, or governed by any preordained rhythm or meter, or bar length. Of course, not all "free Jazz" eschewed all of these elements—but for the first time, players could base their improvisations solely on their own emotional impulses or immediate stimuli of their musical surroundings. But even within this context, there were ties to previous traditions.

There were a number of innovations that occurred in the late '50s that took a few years to have a wide impact: the atonal excursions of pianist Cecil Taylor, the associative, aharmonic yet blueslike music of Ornette Coleman, as well as the modal excursions of Miles Davis, which led to John Coltrane's extended experiments. The Jazz mainstream went through a major retrenchment during these years as it shed the last vestiges of the popular music traditions that had served as its last bridge to wider culture.

At this point, an astonishing group of players and/or composer/bandleaders emerged. Granted, some of them had been around in the '50s, but their moment in the sun came in the '60s. A partial list would include pianists Bill Evans, Herbie

Hancock, Chick Corea, Paul Bley, Keith Jarrett, and Andrew Hill; saxophonists Eric Dolphy, Joe Henderson, Wayne Shorter, and Steve Lacy; trombonists Roswell Rudd and Grachan Moncur III; trumpeters Freddie Hubbard, Booker Little, and Woody Shaw; guitarists Jim Hall and Grant Green; bassists Ron Carter and Gary Peacock; and drummers Elvin Jones, Tony Williams, Beaver Harris, and Paul Motian.

Ornette Coleman's appearance on the Jazz scene and the self-conscious titles of his albums (*The Shape of Jazz to Come, Change of the Century*) conspired to radically alter the status quo of harmonic/melodic variations that had been at Jazz's center since its inception. His music was at once rural and supremely urban. The blues were always audible in his keening saxophone style, but this was the kind of music that was only in demand in the most cosmopolitan of cities and from the most sophisticated of audiences. This, coupled with Coltrane's sudden metamorphosis from an above-average tenor man in the mid-fifties into a leading light of Jazz expression in 1961 threw Rollins (and many others) into a tizzy, and set the mode of Jazz performance that continues to be a dominant force in the music to this day.

After exploring every aspect of diatonic, chromatic, and modal harmony, Coltrane turned to ever more frenetic modes of expression that rendered all previous endeavors obsolete. These were occasionally offset with more ruminative pieces, but in general his music took on a strained quality that made listening to it difficult for some. That was his right as an artist, of course, but this progression had serious consequences for the next few decades. His death in 1967 took Jazz's last undeniable major innovator away, making the subsequent definition of epochs, which had always revolved around an instrumentalist, much harder to quantify.

With the advent of Albert Ayler, Bill Dixon, and others in the mid-sixties, things changed once more. Musicians who were unequipped to deal with the conventions of the past became significant figures. Without making a value judgment as to the merit of their work, this was nonetheless a sea change. Concurrently, both Sun Ra and the Art Ensemble of Chicago were mixing theater with a wide variety of Jazz styles, and contained in their ensembles some musicians who were master improvisers, while others were far more limited, but nonetheless served a function. Groups such as these helped to stratify the declining Jazz public even more, and called into question the whole process by which the music had evolved.

Con-Fusion

As the '60s progressed, the times when young Jazz musicians actually broke through to the general public, as Herbie Hancock had with "Watermelon Man," were rare, indeed. The distance between their music and the general public continued to widen. It was in response to this rift that Miles Davis began experimenting first with electronic instruments and then with increasing doses of rock and funk elements. Confused by their irrelevance to popular culture and the steady withering of work, many musicians followed Davis down the mine-laden road that became fusion music. "Fusion" was named after the blending of Jazz with rock (with more than a dollop of funk thrown in), a mixture that eventually hit a brick wall. The

Sonny's Sabbatical

One of the offshoots of the ascendance of saxophonists John Coltrane and Ornette Coleman in 1959 was Sonny Rollins's taking of a two-year sabbatical. This was virtually unheard of for a major figure at the height of his creative powers and commercial success. Artie Shaw had walked off the bandstand of a New York hotel in late 1939 and gone to Mexico to get his head together, but he was only absent a few months. Rollins entered a period of reflection, practice, and abstinence from performing in public. Rumors began to fly in the Jazz press about what Sonny was up to. A chance encounter with journalist Ralph Berton while Sonny was practicing on New York City's Williamsburg Bridge led to a thinly disguised piece of fiction (the span became the Brooklyn Bridge) in the July 1961 issue of *Metronome*. Shortly thereafter, Rollins announced his comeback—a gig at the Jazz Gallery—and suddenly the Jazz world was awash with anticipation. What would the "new" Sonny sound like? He would answer that question in his album *The Bridge*.

rhythmic bases of the two styles were incompatible, but there is no denying that many creative musicians found the genre enticing. Certainly the electric bassist Jaco Pastorius created many masterpieces tilling these fields, as did a handful of others. Fusion continues today, with many musicians, including young masters such as Joshua Redman, Christian McBride, Russell Gunn, and James Carter, creating new amalgams of contemporary pop trends and the Jazz tradition.

End of the Century

An unprecedented variety of musicians from all of Jazz's generations were professionally active in the '70s and '80s. Never before or since has there been such a wide range of Jazz expression extant. It should not be inferred that just because innovation was assuming a different function than it had before that no great Jazz music was being created in the last quarter century. Every year saw the coming of a new crop of musicians who were mastering the sophisticated tools that a Jazz musician uses while the veterans continued to hone their art. The alto saxophonist/trumpeter Benny Carter, for instance, who had been a vital force as an improviser, composer, and arranger since the late '20s, reappeared in 1976 after a long hiatus playing better than ever and continued to do so for over twenty years. Lee Konitz and Warne Marsh, two extraordinarily creative and original improvisers, shook off to varying degrees the overwhelming influence of Lennie Tristano and appeared with great regularity in clubs and concert halls around the world. Joe Lovano, Wynton Marsalis, Bill Frisell, and Kenny Garrett began to establish themselves as talented youngsters and laid the groundwork for their development into the major figures they are today.

As it became clear that fusion was not going to lead Jazz back to the steady progression of innovation that had been the norm before the mid-sixties, "straight-ahead" playing began to come back into vogue. Expatriate musicians who had been struggling to make ends meet in the States in the '60s were welcomed back as the sophisticated giants they truly were. Tenor saxophonist Dexter Gordon was the first to experience this sudden reversal, and was eventually nominated for an Oscar (Best Actor in the film *Round Midnight*) and featured with the New York Philharmonic. While the experiences of others returning were not quite that sweet, many found work where there had been none before and resettled in their native land.

One of the offshoots of this celebration of Jazz's past was the creation of the repertory orchestras. Many of the musicians who had played in the great bands of the '20s, '30s, and '40s were still professionally active, and they formed the basis for the first wave of bands that appeared in the '70s. George Wein's New York Jazz Repertory Company was one of the first and very best of these bands, as was Chuck Israel's National Jazz Ensemble, which favored a more contemporary reading of the classics. They paved the way for the American Jazz Orchestra, the Smithsonian Jazz Masterworks Orchestra, the Lincoln Center Jazz Orchestra, and the Carnegie Hall Jazz Band, each of which succeeded in establishing its own parameters in dealing with Jazz's heritage.

A handful of the avant-garde's most organized composer/bandleaders—Muhal Richard Abrams, Henry Threadgill, and Julius Hemphill—established themselves as original voices and made many classic recordings, though work was not always forthcoming. And they helped to solidify the burgeoning downtown avant garde scene, which is still a vital part of New York's Jazz life. Marty Erlich, Steve Bernstein, John Zorn, Don Byron, Ben Allison, and others seek out musics from varied cultures and blend them with their own backgrounds to create amalgams that defy categorization. They also reflect the way that Jazz has become a truly international music. Two of Jazz's most individual voices sprang quickly from European musical soil—in the '30s the guitarist Django Reinhardt and in the '50s, the pianist Martial Solal.

But the greatest change in Jazz in terms of its public profile and its musical direction in recent times came under the aegis of Wynton Marsalis. Despite the best intentions of a number of celebrities who identified themselves as big Jazz fans and who tried every so often to do something about the music's relative anonymity with the American public, Marsalis was able to capture the interest of a large enough segment of the population to start a Jazz renaissance of sorts. To begin with, he is a gifted educator, and throughout his many travels has managed to encourage and mentor hundreds of young aspiring players. More than a few of these have turned into top-flight artists, and they in turn have been carrying the educational torch to the next generation. As the artistic director of Jazz at Lincoln Center, he has overseen a burgeoning program with a strong educational bent that is unlike anything in the music's history. There has been controversy, to be sure, but then what large organization in or out of the arts has not had its share of that? As an improviser and composer, Marsalis has evolved steadily from his days in Art Blakey's band into one of the major voices of his generation.

Jazz at the Millennium

As we get deeper into this new century, there are many new voices on the horizon that bode well for the future of the music. Among the freshest are the trumpeters Dave Douglas and Marcus Printup; the saxophonists Mark Turner, Scott

Robinson, Kris Bauman, and Dayna Sean Stephens; the guitarist Kurt Rosenwinkel; the pianist Eric Reed; the drummers Leon Parker and Jason Brown; viabraphonist Warren Wolf; and the bassists Christian McBride and Avishai Cohen. It is also no longer the exception, but the rule, that the best non-American musicians are on an even step with the American ones. Virtually every country in which Jazz has developed—be it Norway, Hungary, Japan, or any number of African and Latin American nations—has its own traditions and its unique amalgam of musical influences. They, too, are much deserving of our attention.

Although it is convenient to divide Jazz history into neat eras and attach catchphrases to them, the music's evolution is far more complex. Furthermore, these labels are sabotaged by shared influences, intricate crosscurrents, and many singular figures whose music defies pigeonholing. As far back as 1957, the noted pianist/educator Billy Taylor wrote: " 'Semantics' has become a fashionable word of late. And nowhere is the word more overused than in Jazz circles, where all kinds of semantic acrobatics are being performed by self-styled experts, critics, and other writers on Jazz. Frankly, the semantics of Jazz annoy me! Such words as *hot, bop, progressive, funky, East Coast*, and *West Coast* mean one thing to one person and something else to another. Actually, these labels have done much to confuse the public about Jazz." We can now add forty-five years later that their adoption by Jazz education has succeeded in confusing generations of Jazz students about the relationships between the various eras of Jazz.

And no less a figure than Benny Carter, who has been a creative force in Jazz for nine decades, has consistently expressed dissatisfaction with the term *jazz* itself: "I don't object to the word *jazz* because I feel it is a pejorative term. I object to it because it has become meaningless. Any single word that attempts to encompass everything from ragtime to swing, Louis Armstrong, Ornette Coleman, Sun Ra, and Harry Connick, Jr., has to be meaningless."

Finally, Jazz has evolved in a relatively short time, so that even its earliest styles continued to be played (often by their creators) throughout all segments of its history. For example, in 1960, you could hear Louis Armstrong, Earl Hines, Coleman Hawkins, Duke Ellington, Pee Wee Russell, Benny Carter, Benny Goodman, Count Basie, Charles Mingus, Miles Davis, Thelonious Monk, John Coltrane, Bill Evans, Ornette Coleman, Cecil Taylor, and Eric Dolphy. What is astounding today was just matter-of-fact then. While we are charting the innovations that defined the new sounds of the era, it is worth remembering that the best of the veterans kept listening to the new music and the best of the young titans also heard their elders—and they all reflected one another.

THREE

Varieties of Jazz

To break down as protean an art form as Jazz into a series of "varieties" makes for a daunting challenge. Every attempt to define a particular school is almost at once subverted by the similarities to music that came before and music that came after. And in a music as individualistic as Jazz, it is hard to find many players who can consistently be said to subscribe to any one particular set of precepts.

Especially since the 1960s, the potential for Jazz artists mixing and matching the best of the past with the new has experienced exponential growth. Furthermore, as Jazz has gained status around the globe, performers of all stripes have freely integrated Jazz elements into their own musics. Out of this symbiosis, many genres have evolved that bear little relation to Jazz's American roots. This speaks to the vital power of Jazz, and it should be welcomed.

The time may well be approaching to abandon all the categories and just refer to music by the person who played it. After all, "bop" is much too large an umbrella to cover the music of Parker, Gillespie, Monk, and Dameron.

Still, for better or worse, the history and attendant styles of Jazz have long been canonized into a sequence that is too deeply entrenched to be ignored. So for those who would like a hand in wending their way through the lexicon of Jazz styles, here goes.

Bop: All music is tied to its cultural context, and bop (also known as bebop) is inextricably bound to the social issues of the early 1940s, when young black musicians defined themselves against the pernicious remnants of minstrelsy that were buried deep in popular culture. Not only did they behave differently, but their music, in the context of its time, had a penchant for dissonance that many found off-putting. Gone, for the most part, were the straightforward melodies that distinguished the best of the American popular song. Unlike previous styles of Jazz, much of bop seemed to have a "take it or leave it" attitude when it came to mass appeal. And in this regard, it aligned itself with other contemporary forms of art in other genres. This, of course, played into the hands of both audiences—those seeking to be "hip" and into something new, and those who liked to feel excluded.

Bop was basically an instrumental music, though it did have its vocal subgenre (with even more nonsense syllables and affectations than the worst excesses of the Swing Era).

The rhythm sections played in a more overtly aggressive fashion than before, with the drummer tending to predominate, shaping the general flow of the accompaniment. The bop vocabulary was largely taken verbatim from the solos of saxophonist Charlie Parker and trumpeter Dizzy Gillespie, and reveled in angular melodic shapes ("Shaw 'Nuff" and "Salt Peanuts").

These solos were characterized by a great range, clean and virtuosic displays of technique, a penchant for unresolved chord changes, and a sense of great urgency. This is not to imply that these characteristics are also not to be found in earlier music—of course they are—but it's a matter of proportion. And in the same way that it took awhile for Armstrong's innovation to trickle down to the next generation, many of the first attempts to capture Parker's and Gillespie's style were immature. Among the first to deal effectively with their new music were the trumpeters Miles Davis and Fats Navarro, the trombonist J. J. Johnson, the tenor saxophonists Wardell Gray and Sonny Rollins, the pianists Bud Powell and Dodo Marmarosa, the vibraphonist Milt Jackson, the bassists Oscar Pettiford and Charles Mingus, and the drummers Max Roach and Roy Haynes.

Bop was essentially a small-group music (though Gillespie valiantly tried to sustain a big band for several years) played by a couple of horns and a rhythm section of piano, bass, and drums. There was little in the way of arrangements or interludes—once the theme was stated, a string of solos followed, with the theme being restated without variation at the end. With this eschewing of the compositional and ensemble element, a much greater demand was placed on the individual soloists. Few of the acolytes of Parker and Gillespie had a comparable genius and most could not sustain interest over long periods of time. But those who could brought a new electricity and risk taking to the music that could be thrilling. It is a decidedly unsentimental music, but bop in its most concentrated form does not lack for a want of emotion.

There were those who blended the best of the Swing Era with the new vocabulary, and they tended to be composer/arrangers. Tadd Dameron and Gil Evans found ways to weave the new sounds into arrangements that restored some of the balance between the ensemble and the soloist. In many ways, their music formed a bridge between the aggressive extremes of some of the early bop music and the cool Jazz that was to follow.

Bossa Nova: During the early 1960s, in the waning days of the pre-Beatles music world, there were a few bright moments when popular music approached the kind of sophistication that had been taken for granted in the '30s and early '40s. The bossa nova craze of the '60s was one of those moments. It was led by a handful of young composers and instrumentalists in South America who, inspired by pianist and composer Gerry Mulligan and other Jazz writers, strove to combine the best of modern Jazz with their own rhythmically propulsive native music. In the late '50s, the partnership of guitarist/singer Joao Gilberto and composer Antonio Carlos Jobim created quite a stir in Brazil with their collaboration on "Chega de Saudade."

The rhythms were descendants of the Brazilian samba, and it was frequently accented by the use of acoustic guitars.

Though there were intimations of things to come and an intersection between Jazz and Brazilian music, it wasn't until the American guitarist Charlie Byrd asked saxophonist Stan Getz to record the now classic album *Jazz Samba* that bossa nova ("new wave" in Portuguese) was launched. Getz became an international attraction based on his subsequent albums, with his biggest hit being Jobim's "The Girl from Impanema." The intimate, almost spoken vocal by Gilberto's wife, Astrud, played a large role in the success of this recording.

Though its popularity has waned, there remains a large audience for bossa nova, and it continues to occupy a significant place in the Jazz marketplace. Two outstanding albums in the genre are Stan Getz's *Big Band Bossa* and saxophonist Wayne Shorter's *Native Dancer* (with Milton Nascimento).

Chicago Jazz: The presence of New Orleans masters in Chicago in the '20s such as King Oliver, Louis Armstrong, and the Dodds Brothers (clarinetist Johnny and drummer Baby) had a profound influence on a group of young, white musicians who wanted to find their own Jazz voices. Their efforts reflected the heady atmosphere of their hometown, rather than the blues-inspired reflections of Oliver and company. The most significant fact about the Austin High Gang (some of them attended that institution) was that their role models were African Americans. Out of this group came the clarinetists Frank Teschemacher and Benny Goodman; drummers Dave Tough, Gene Krupa, and George Wettling; and the cornetist Muggsy Spanier. (Black youngsters like drummers Sidney Catlett and Lionel Hampton and bassist Milt Hinton were also there in Chicago, picking up from the same men—but are conveniently overlooked by those who used the term "Chicago Jazz.")

In later years, the bandleader/guitarist Eddie Condon became the personification of the Chicago school. He had a quick wit—and about the boppers, he said, "They flat their fifths; we drink ours")—and generated a lot of work for a long time. But nonetheless, this style remained confining for the handful of superlative players who were its prime exponents. Musicians such as Pee Wee Russell, Roy Eldridge, Buck Clayton, Bud Freeman, Vic Dickenson, George Wettling, and many others spent the great majority of their later careers unfairly grouped in this category. On the rare occasions when these musicians were given the latitude to expand on a more varied repertoire with musicians of different stylistic stripes, the results were generally revelatory.

Cool Jazz: "Cool" is the term used to refer to the reaction to bop, in which its frequently frenetic tempos and impassioned solos were replaced by a more reflective attitude. This was usually expressed in moderate tempos and in an instrumental style that drew heavily on the example of the great saxophonist Lester Young, though it must be stated that in lesser hands, Young's style was occasionally distorted beyond recognition. Nonetheless, cool Jazz was a welcome relief to the rapid degeneration of the bop style in inferior hands. And in the hands of masters such as trumpeter Miles Davis, baritone saxophonist Gerry Mulligan, and pianist Dave Brubeck, it was a thing of great beauty.

The origins of the style, which emerged in the late 1940s,

may be traced to Claude Thornhill's big band, an ensemble which favored clarinets, French horns, and tuba. Many young musicians (who had revolved around saxophonist Charlie Parker and trumpeter Dizzy Gillespie) were attracted to this sonority and to the innovative arrangements Gil Evans wrote for the band, adapting elements from classical music to Jazz ends.

With Davis as the primary force, Evans and others (trumpeter John Carisi, pianist John Lewis, and baritone saxophonist Mulligan) arrived at a band of their own that used the smallest amount of instruments necessary to get the tonal colors they desired—trumpet, trombone, alto sax, baritone sax, French horn, tuba, piano, bass, and drums. The solos were integrated into the ensemble in an Ellingtonian fashion, and this forced the players to think compositionally ("Boplicity," "Moon Dreams," and "Jeru"). The band's dynamic range was wide, but the group never shouted, and functioned best at a medium to medium-soft level that let all the instruments shine. Though the band was a commercial flop and folded shortly after its debut, its recordings (originally 78s) were reissued the year after as an early LP, titled *The Birth of the Cool*—and the name stuck.

In the next few years, virtually any new Jazz style that was not overtly boplike was classified as cool. This rather large umbrella covered the music of Lennie Tristano, Dave Brubeck, and Mulligan, all of whom, like the *Birth of the Cool* musicians, shared Lester Young as an inspiration—but each of whom came up with radically different results. Yes, there was a surface placidity to the sound of their bands, and in relation to Parker and Gillespie, maybe they were "cool," but that's as far as it goes.

Dixieland Jazz: Most of the misinformation that has befallen New Orleans Jazz comes from what has become known as "Dixieland" Jazz. Here the emphasis was on banjos, straw hats, a clipped and frequently unswinging way of phrasing, and hokum. In the mid-forties, a group of white musicians on the West Coast began replicating the music of cornetist King Oliver and others, and this led a "New Orleans" revival—the primary exponent of which was a band led by Lu Watters. Their efforts, though occasionally amateurish, were sincere and respectful of their music's roots. Their popularity led to a whole genre of Dixieland Jazz, which seemed dedicated to exploiting the surface elements of nostalgia while ignoring the artistic essence at the heart of the music they were celebrating. In its most commercial incarnations, Dixieland was, in essence, another aspect of minstrelsy in that it was based on a distortion of an African-American idiom. And even in its more benign forms, it remained a prison of sorts for many superlative players.

Free Jazz: This phenomenon of the late '50s and '60s was the ultimate reaction not only to the complexities of bop, but of all the Jazz that preceded it. Free Jazz—also called avant garde—gave up on functional harmony altogether, relying instead on a far ranging, stream-of-consciousness approach to melodic variation. Saxophonist Ornette Coleman was the fount of inspiration of this genre. This is not to say that there weren't other attempts to get rid of chords before he came along, but it was the way that Coleman did it that caught on. To begin with, he was a superb blues player and his band always swung. His melodies varied from abstractions on Charlie Parker to yearning ballads and blues. As the '60s progressed, Coleman's discoveries opened the floodgates to all sorts of improvised music that was called free Jazz. While some of it was fascinating, for the most part it was a freedom that was unearned and that freed the players from nothing—except, as some noted, from playing for free. One musician likened free Jazz to playing tennis without a net. But Coleman's music was rich in mood, and his band could always be counted on for a series of classic improvisations.

There was another stream of musicians who were associated directly or indirectly with the later bands of saxophonist John Coltrane, who took up free Jazz. Coltrane had been immensely affected by Coleman's music, but when he played "free," it had a very different feeling. As he neared his early death in 1967, one got the impression that Coltrane's music was functioning more and more as an emotional catharsis, and it became increasingly difficult to assess by any of the standards used for previous Jazz musics. But what made it endlessly fascinating was his background and what he was choosing *not* to play as much as what he did play.

There was a rash of saxophonists pursuing different aspects of free Jazz in the '60s, most notably Albert Ayler and Archie Shepp. Their approaches were radically different, though: Ayler frequently conjured mystical moments of religious possession, sounding like he was speaking in tongues on his tenor saxophone, while Shepp, an intellectual, courted the fringe of more traditional forms while remaining outside them.

Slightly later, Anthony Braxton and Chicago's Association for the Advancement of Creative Musicians (AACM) came on the scene, each with idiosyncratic takes on the Jazz tradition that incorporated theater and a healthy sense of humor into their (at times) searing reflections on contemporary society.

Fusion: As many have noted, Jazz was born out of a melding of styles, but this term has come to stand for the blending of Jazz with rock and funk. It happened in the late '60s, and was inevitable. Jazz had always had a healthy audience amongst the young, and as younger Jazz players who were weaned on rock came of age, they began to experiment with "fusions" of both. The figure who made it acceptable for the Jazz establishment was trumpeter Miles Davis, who was the prime instigator and undeniably the major factor in this music's initial appeal.

The album that inarguably created the genre was Davis's 1969 effort, *Bitches Brew*, and in many ways it remains unsurpassed. The problem that plagued most of the subsequent fusion music was that the basis of rock rhythms is essentially static, and without the forward motion of Jazz rhythm, the music loses its profile. This is not to say that all Jazz has to be played atop a swinging 4/4 beat, but when it is altogether absent, the issue of determining the music's provenance can get sticky.

One of the most creative and prolific fusion bands was Weather Report, which featured former Davis alumni saxophonist Wayne Shorter and pianist Joe Zawinul. They brought to their explorations a solid musical background and sense of swing that carried over into whatever they did. The electric bassist/composer Jaco Pastorius came to fame in this band and became a figure analogous to Charles Mingus in his ability to take anything he liked and find a place for it in his music. He was also, like Mingus, a true virtuoso on his instrument who changed the way the electric bass would be played in the future.

Keyboard player Herbie Hancock's Headhunters band of the early '70s looked to soul, funk, and R&B more than rock for its rhythmic base, and became extraordinarily successful. His recording of "Chameleon" was a huge hit and was covered by many artists. Other outstanding groups include Return to Forever and John McLaughlin's Mahavishnu Orchestra, whose profile was closer to rock than the others, but which nonetheless made some very creative albums early on. The novelty generated by the juxtapositions that created fusion wore off quickly, and by the 1980s it became a commercial music with little to recommend it to serious Jazz listeners. One of the few groups to take the genre seriously has been pianist Chick Corea's Elektric Band, whose late '80s and early '90s recordings have yet to be challenged as the most recent fusion milestones.

Hard Bop: Like cool Jazz, hard bop was a reaction to bop. In 1953, drummer Art Blakey and pianist Horace Silver sought to capture a part of the listening and dancing audience that had been "lost" by bop's fast tempos and sheer virtuosity. They managed this by slowing down most of the tempos, using elements of earlier Jazz styles mixed with elements of church music, and making a concerted attempt to reach the lay black population that had abandoned modern Jazz for

R&B and soul music. If West Coast Jazz was largely white players in California, hard bop was largely East Coast African Americans. Hard bop also brought back some elements from the Swing Era, with arrangements that had interludes, introductions, vamps, and other devices to add an important element of counterpoint. Classic albums include Blakey's *Moanin'* and Silver's *Song for My Father*.

Hard bop was played for the most part by two or three horns (trumpet, tenor sax, trombone) plus rhythm section. And an interesting thing began to take place in the late '50s as Blakey and Silver continued to hire the best young players around. They naturally were keeping up to date with the newest bits of musical information filtering down from John Coltrane, Sonny Rollins, and others, and there resulted a wonderful contrast between the rather basic, foursquare repertoire, and solos that went further and further afield in their explorations. It is a credit to Blakey in particular that he encouraged this sort of experimentation and gave his bandsmen the opportunity to contribute their own music to the band's library. By the early '60s, with trumpeter Freddie Hubbard and saxophonist Wayne Shorter in his band, he produced albums such as *Free for All* that are as hard swinging as they are experimental.

One of hard bop's most brilliant exponents was saxophonist Cannonball Adderley, who after reaching the pinnacle of the Jazz world as a member of Miles Davis's band in the late '50s, formed a quintet with his brother, cornetist Nat. A gifted raconteur and bandleader, Adderley found a rare intersection of commercialism and art that made him a leading figure of the '60s right up through his early death in 1975 at age forty-six. His 1966 hit recording of "Mercy, Mercy, Mercy" expanded the populist tendencies of hard bop right into "soul Jazz."

Kansas City Swing: Kansas City was to the '20s and '30s what New Orleans had been to the 1900s and 1910s. The town was wide open, and the music took on the characteristics of both its rural and urban nature. Kansas City swing was based in the blues, yet approached it with a newfound sophistication.

In the mid-thirties, bassist Walter Page, after years as the leader of his own band and the linchpin of another (Bennie Moten's), found himself in the rhythm section of Count Basie's band. Page soon managed to translate his own swinging beat to the other members of the section. Together, they created a four-man unit that played as one. They swung hard, but with a light touch and elegance that was new to Jazz. This enabled the best of the Kansas City horn players to play with the tempo in a new fashion. Lester Young, the most brilliant of these, helped make the Basie band one of the best of the era. They went to New York in December 1936, and within a short time, both Benny Goodman—who, along with his brother-in-law, producer John Hammond, had been responsible for getting the band out of KC—and Duke Ellington became fans.

Other groups that reflected the Kansas City magic and that made the successful trek eastward to New York were Andy Kirk and his Clouds of Joy and Jay McShann's band, which brought Charlie Parker onto the national Jazz scene. One of the founding fathers of R&B, which led directly to rock and roll, was the singer Big Joe Turner, who began his career as a singing bartender at Piney Brown's legendary KC saloon.

Latin Jazz: West Indian, Caribbean, and Spanish music were all essential ingredients in the formation of Jazz in New Orleans. Early blues hits such as the "St. Louis Blues" had a "tango" chorus, and many of Jelly Roll Morton's pieces referenced these rhythms. A major turning point occurred in 1930 when a recording of a rhumba, "El Manisero," known as "The Peanut Vendor," became the first Afro-Cuban dance to become popular with the American public at large. Both Louis Armstrong and Duke Ellington quickly recorded their own versions, and both continued to explore Afro-Cuban pieces throughout the '30s. Indeed, Juan Tizol, a Puerto Rican trombonist who was in Ellington's band for more than twenty years, composed "Perdido," "Caravan," "Moonlight Fiesta," "Conga Brava," and "Bakiff" for the band. But the big breakthrough that cleared the way for a new idiom that was equally Afro-Cuban and Jazz came about through the efforts of multiinstrumentalist/arranger Mario Bauza. A classically trained Cuban musician, he played first with Chick Webb's band, and then, while working with Cab Calloway in 1939, met the young trumpeter Dizzy Gillespie, who showed a big interest in the subtleties of Afro-Cuban music.

When Gillespie formed his own big band in the midforties, Bauza (by this time a key figure in Machito's Afro-Cuban band) introduced him to the legendary *conguero* Chano Pozo. This turned out to be a historic, though short-lived association (Pozo was killed in a barroom brawl shortly after).

Together, they recorded the first Latin Jazz masterpieces ("Cubano Be," "Cubano Bop," and "Manteca") in 1947. Other bands were also exploring the same territory, most notably Stan Kenton ("The Peanut Vendor" and "Cuban Episode"). By the early '50s, Machito's band was featuring Charlie Parker, Gillespie, and others as guest soloists, and Latin Jazz was well on the way to becoming an established genre.

As the '50s went on, there was a tremendous amount of diversity among the bandleaders working in the Latin Jazz arena (aficionados actually prefer the term "Afro-Cuban Jazz"). Tito Puente, who besides being a wonderful vibraphonist was a skilled and original arranger, led a high quality band for years. His music eventually became famous as salsa, a commercial term for which he had great disdain (it means "sauce") but there was no fighting it.

The brothers Charlie and Eddie Palmieri have managed the miracle of being both popular (in the Latin community, at least) and tremendously artistic since the 1960s. Both are respected within the genre as truly brilliant musicians. Pianist Eddie is an experimental pianist/arranger who is almost a Monklike figure in Latin Jazz—one of his greatest albums is *The Sun of Latin Music*. Mongo Santamaria, a legendary Cuban *conguero* like Pozo, had the greatest commercial success in the genre with "Watermelon Man" in the early '60s. In recent years, Cuban musicians have been able to emigrate to the U.S. on occasion.

Modal Jazz: A mode is a musical scale. The most common ones are the ones formed in an octave's range by using only the piano's white keys. In modal Jazz, the improvisers use these scales instead of chords as the fodder for their solos. This gives the music a more "horizontal" sound, but it also creates a sense of tonal rigidity that can become at least as trying on listeners as can too many chords. But, in the hands of pianist Bill Evans, trumpeter Miles Davis, saxophonist John Coltrane, or pianist George Russell, modal Jazz provided a new avenue of expression for players who needed a break from the well-worn musical vocabulary.

While there had been premonitions of and experiments with modal Jazz before, Miles Davis's 1959 *Kind of Blue* brought it to a large audience with a handful of classic performances. Some of the soloists did not limit themselves exclusively to the modes when improvising, but the modal basis of some of the compositions is what made them sound so different. Another vital component in the success of this recording was that all of the players were past masters at the intricacies of diatonic Jazz harmony and brought their mastery of that idiom into their modal explorations. Later improvisers, who had not had that experience, were not able to distinguish themselves melodically in the modal idiom, and this created a glut of rather uninspired performances. John Coltrane's "Impressions" and Davis's "So What" are quintessential modal pieces, with simple, scalar melodies. This style presented a particular challenge to the guitarists, pianists, and vibraphonists, who could not fall back on their usual voicings and progressions without sounding anachronistic.

New Orleans Jazz: The classic formation of trumpet, clarinet, trombone, piano, guitar or banjo, tuba or bass, and drums has come to represent the definitive New Orleans Jazz band, though any number and variety of instruments can play the music. What is usually referred to as "New Orleans Jazz" grew out of the rich musical and cultural heritage of its cosmopolitan home. Its emergence after World War I was the product of many influences. One of the most significant came from the band orchestrations of ragtime music that flowered around the country in the early twentieth century. The players began to improvise within the framework of these arrangements, and from this came the rough and tumble and spontaneous form that evolved quickly into what became known as Jazz in the mid-1910s.

There are many explanations for precisely how this occurred and which musicians were the key movers. Buddy Bolden's 1905 band seems to have been a prime factor in spreading a new kind of blues-based instrumental music around New Orleans that was soon to be developed by the next generation of players. But what we do know from the first definitive recordings of the genre, those made in 1923 by King Oliver's Creole Jazz Band, is that a generation of musicians had arrived at a miraculous way of playing together and generating a rocking and rolling music (with a swinging 4/4 beat and a basis in the blues). Their conception remains at the root of Jazz to this day.

New Orleans Jazz is basically contrapuntal in nature, meaning different melodies play off against one another at the same time. Although solos play a part in it, the essence of the music is transmitted by the confluence of many people playing at the same time, without getting in one another's way. In fact, not only do they not step on one another's musical toes, but much of the magic comes from the brushes and rubs that occur between the instruments. In this sense, each player is a composer of his own line in a spontaneously created composition. This eventually led to the liberation of one of the lines into a preeminent solo, and it was to this task that Louis Armstrong applied his genius. He was at once the quintessential New Orleans musician and the one who brought about the next era in the music's evolution. Because of its ensemble nature, New Orleans Jazz stayed firmly rooted to the piece at hand, and the solos tended to be melodic paraphrases that eventually grew into variations. It was from this that Armstrong's brilliance emerged and eventually made the variations themselves the goal.

The 1923 King Oliver Creole Jazz Band (on which Armstrong recorded his first solos) and the 1926 Jelly Roll Morton Red Hot Peppers sessions represent the joys of New Orleans Jazz and reveal the tremendous variety of approaches to be found within the idiom. No matter how different their music may sound, what unites them is that all of the instrumentalists were playing the great majority of the time, and yet their music never sounds cluttered.

So in its myriad expressions of form, New Orleans Jazz has far more variety than most subsequent styles of Jazz. The great composers—Ellington, Lewis, Mingus, Brookmeyer, Marsalis among them—never forgot this and leavened their music with similar alternations of structure.

Bands made up of older players from New Orleans, led by the clarinetist George Lewis and the Preservation Hall Jazz Band, enjoyed great success from the 1950s on. While they were regarded as "authentic," they were comprised largely of second-rank musicians, and this gave New Orleans music a primitive profile in the minds of many. This was followed by the more refined efforts of pianist Bob Greene in the '60s and '70s, which were well-received. However, it was the emergence of trumpeter Wynton Marsalis in the 1980s and his championing of the real roots and relevance of the genre that brought worldwide exposure to the glories of New Orleans Jazz. He made it live and breathe without even a whiff of antiquarianism. Consequently, it is no longer the exception, but the rule, for young players to be conversant in its vernacular, and that is a wonderful thing to see.

Smooth Jazz: Smooth Jazz is really a subset of fusion, but it has gained such a tremendous profile in the last decade that it deserves its own heading. It is basically an easy-listening genre. Musicians of all different stripes have ventured into this genre, from the immensely talented Jazz guitarist George Benson and the big bandleader Bob Mintzer (he is a key member of The Yellowjackets) to saxophonists Kenny G., Najee, and Dave Koz. Perhaps the musician who did more to create the idiom than anyone, saxophonist Grover Washington, Jr., was competent in the Jazz language and used his knowledge of it to enlighten his forays into lighter-weight music. His protégés, however, rarely have his talent or his feeling for the blues.

Soul Jazz: In the 1960s, soul Jazz took hard bop one step further in its pursuit of a young, urban crowd, and reduced the complexities of bop even further. It was not unusual for there to be a repeated loop of a bassline as the "hook" for a piece. To be sure, this had been used in many other styles of Jazz before, but again, it was a matter of emphasis. Whereas hard bop's Art Blakey kept in touch with the new sounds of Jazz through the sidemen he chose, pianist Horace Silver played up the "funky" nature of his music and influenced a whole generation of musicians, some of whom brought big hits to other bands, including pianist Bobby Timmons's classic, "Moanin,' " for the Blakey band.

Then there was the appearance of the organist Jimmy Smith in the mid-fifties, and his string of hit albums that merged his mastery of the Charlie Parker idiom with a penchant for "soul" and vestiges of R&B. The blues (as a form, not as an inspiration) played a much larger role in soul Jazz than it had in hard bop, and organ trios with guitar and drums popped up in clubs around the country. Out of this milieu came major talents like the guitarists George Benson and Grant Green; the organists Shirley Scott, Jimmy McGriff, and Richard "Groove" Holmes; and the saxophonists Stanley Turrentine and Eddie Harris. Back when Jazz was part of the mainstream of popular music, Armstrong, Ellington, and others could create works that had the potential to satisfy listeners who came to the music expecting sheer commercialism or sheer art (or any combination thereof). By the time soul Jazz became a commodity in the mid-sixties, the vestiges of Jazz and R&B were fighting a losing battle against the encroaching hegemony of rock and roll, then in its English incarnation. Although some of it is quite commendable, little of soul Jazz has attained "classic" status in the pantheon of Jazz.

Stride: This two-handed approach to Jazz piano is based in a strong, steady accompaniment in the left hand, which alternates between a low bass note and an answering chord played an octave or so higher. It is the effort taken to make these sometimes difficult jumps that led to the name "stride." The right hand generally carries the melodic lead. The great challenge is to take on this "Handful of Keys" (which is the name of a stride composition by Fats Waller) and make it swing. This is a virtuoso's music, since the essential nature of this piano style is orchestral. Counterpoint, shifts of rhythm and register, somehow have to be accomplished not by horns, but by manipulation of ten fingers. And while the essential horn players of early Jazz were based in New Orleans, the men who invented Jazz piano for the most part wound up in and around New York City.

The ragtime pianists Eubie Blake and Luckey Roberts were great virtuosi and songwriters, and their stretching of ragtime's limits during the 1910s pointed toward a new style. James P. Johnson, who picked up where they left off, has rightly been called the "father of stride piano," and from his innovations of the early 1920s flowed the great majority of Jazz piano styles. Whereas ragtime was not an improvised music, Johnson became known for his ability to spin off variations on a theme that lasted for thirty minutes and more. His early recorded solos and piano rolls (most notably "Carolina Shout") became the basic text that taught Duke Ellington and countless others how to make a piano swing. And through Johnson's disciple Thomas "Fats" Waller, we get a direct link to Count Basie. Waller was an even more refined pianist than Johnson, and while he composed many hit tunes and became a huge star, in artistic terms, he operated within the idiom that Johnson created. Another seminal figure was

Willie "The Lion" Smith, who was more interested in harmonic variations than the others, and this was also to have a big influence on Ellington.

What all these men shared was an ability to generate a massive sense of swing from the steady beat of their left hands and the relentless melodic variations of their right. Because they frequently had to play for large groups of people, with no one else on the bandstand and no amplification, they were known for their larger-than-life personalities and great showmanship. And though they have been few and far between, there have been players who have mastered this demanding tradition down though the decades. Don Ewell managed to be very creative while staying squarely in the idiom. Thelonious Monk's music was rooted in a brilliantly original abstraction of stride piano. (It's worth noting he knew James P. Johnson and liked to be told he sounded like him on occasion!) And it is only a hop, skip, and a jump from Monk to contemporary Jazz piano, so the link to the stride tradition remains vital. In recent years, Marcus Roberts has come up with some startling and swinging updates of this heritage.

Swing: It took awhile for the young Jazz musicians of the '20s and early '30s to catch up with Louis Armstrong. When they did, and used his language as the basis for their own discoveries, they created what has become known as the "swing" style. This came to fruition when not only the soloists, but the rhythm sections (as a unit) and the big bands (as an ensemble) learned to play with Armstrong's rhythmic feeling and phrasing. The Count Basie rhythm section was the first to perfect this approach, with all four instruments blending into a cohesive whole greater than the sum of its parts. To be sure, there were other players and writers who also contributed, but there is no denying that it was Armstrong's transformative example that served as the prime catalyst for what followed: one of those serendipitous moments when popular culture merged with a new and rapidly expanding art form, with both elements taking inspiration from the other.

Also, the interaction of the swing style with dancers cannot be overstated. As the popular dances that had their roots in the black community became more popular (a trend going back to the early twentieth century), the dancers and the swing musicians looked to each other for inspiration. This helped fuel both groups, as well as the third group that simply liked to listen and watch.

Pianists Teddy Wilson and Count Basie; saxophonists Coleman Hawkins, Lester Young, and Benny Carter; clarinetist Benny Goodman; trumpeter Roy Eldridge; trombonists Jack Teagarden and Dickey Wells; drummers Jo Jones and Sid Catlett; bassist Walter Page; and xylophonist Red Norvo were among the best of this generation. They could sail along at any tempo, skillfully encounter difficult harmonies, deal with the blues in an original fashion, and create solos of any length that were immaculately coherent and original.

The standard formation for their music was the big band. The bands of Count Basie, Benny Goodman, Jimmie Lunceford, Claude Thornhill, and Duke Ellington were certainly different from one another, but they also had much in common. They found a way to organize a large section of horns supported by a rhythm section that sustained an equilibrium between the composed elements and the spontaneous, improvised portions. Each band varied the proportions, but all of these groups followed the same general formula much of the time: The ensemble would play the melody, with spots left open for the leader to help the public readily identify whose band it was; solos or a vocal followed, with the accompaniment being a reduction of Armstronglike phrases, played by one of, or a combination of, the horn sections. There might be a modulation, or an interlude, another solo, and then the climactic out choruses, usually featuring a high-note trumpet or clarinet.

While there were countless variations on this, this is the basic way these bands presented their music. The arrangers, who composed the music the bands played, maintained the same compositional thread that bound New Orleans Jazz. But since they had more instruments at their disposal, and the harmonic base of the music had continued to expand, they had more options.

The greatest soloists of the Swing Era needed an outlet for their Jazz playing where they could "stretch out," and most of them either formed small groups of their own or established combos that alternated with the larger group. Basie's Kansas City 6's and 7's ("Lester Leaps In" and "Dickie's Dream"), the various Goodman chamber groups ("After You've Gone," "Dizzy Spells," and "Body and Soul"), the Ellington units under his sidemen's names ("C Blues," "Love in My Heart," and "Menelik"), and Chick Webb's Chicks ("Stompin' at the Savoy" and "I Got Rhythm") all made many classic recordings. There were a handful of small bands that existed by themselves, the most notable of which was the John Kirby Sextet. Its music was at once accessible and inveterately smart, and its popularity led to its becoming the first black band to have its own network radio spots.

Third Stream: Jazz has been in dialogue with European classical music since its inception. The stride pianists, for instance, would often take a well-known classical piece and "jazz" it by changing the rhythms and improvising on it (this was also an aspect of ragtime). Composer/arrangers such as Bill Challis, Eddie Sauter, Billy Strayhorn, Paul Jordan, and Bob Graettinger found original ways to integrate elements taken directly from classical orchestral music into their own Jazz idioms.

But third stream as a discrete phenomenon was the brainchild of French hornist/composer/conductor Gunther Schuller. Thoroughly at home in any musical genre, Schuller sought in the mid-fifties to combine various elements of these disparate musics—the result of which would be a style without boundaries. As he put it at the time, "It is a way of making music which holds that *all musics are created equal*, coexisting in a beautiful brotherhood/sisterhood of musics that complement and fructify each other. . . . And it is the logical outcome of the American melting pot: *E pluribus unum*."

Most of the classics of third stream came shortly after Schuller coined the term in 1957. Works by George Russell ("All About Rosie"), John Lewis ("Three Little Feelings" and "Golden Striker"), J. J. Johnson ("Jazz Suite for Brass"), and Bill Russo ("An Image of Man") managed to skirt the misunderstandings that eventually doom many artistic crosscultural amalgams.

Although it is little remembered today, Schuller helped John Lewis form the ambitious Orchestra U.S.A. in 1962. It lasted for three years, during the course of which they commissioned Harold Farberman (who was one of the cofounders), Jimmy Guiffre, Hall Overton, Gary McFarland, Benny Golson, and Teo Macero among others. The band itself comprised many first-call Jazz and classical players, and the featured artists included Ornette Coleman, Coleman Hawkins, and Gerry Mulligan. With all this music, it seems all the more strange that Orchestra U.S.A.'s recordings have been largely out of print since the '60s.

Only a few adherents to the third-stream philosophy remain, most notably the pianist/educator Ron Blake. But at the turn of the new century, the genre clearly seems to have prefigured "World Music." Here, we find room for the challenging admixtures of musical cultures that clarinetist Don Byron, saxophonists Steve Coleman and John Zorn, trumpeter Dave Douglas, and guitarist Bill Frisell have created.

West Coast Jazz: Of all the labels out there, this is one of the most misleading. For although many of these players did live on the West Coast, most of them were not born there; the music they played had its roots solidly on the East Coast. Furthermore, there were many different groups of musicians playing on the West Coast whose playing doesn't fit into this category. Nevertheless, it is a movement that has established its own canon. The musicians identified with this style were almost exclusively white, although their prime inspirations remained black players, many of whom were not doing nearly as well in the business as their white counterparts. This created a series of personal and critical schisms that made objective evaluations of their music difficult.

West Coast Jazz is a subgenre of cool Jazz. Players who had been in the Stan Kenton and Woody Herman bands—trumpeter Shorty Rogers, reedman Jimmy Guiffre, drummer Shelly Manne—experimented throughout the 1950s with a wide range of compositional devices that succeeded more often than not, and offered a welcome contrast to the theme-solos-theme bop formula. The various-sized groups led by pianist Gerry Mulligan (most famously his quartet with trumpeter Chet Baker) and saxophonist Stan Getz were also thought to be part of this West Coast crew, though their music related equally to the New Orleans/Kansas City stylings of Lester Young and the Basie small bands and to Charlie Parker.

The basic sound of West Coast Jazz came directly out of the Miles Davis Nonet and the *Birth of the Cool* recordings. The dynamics were kept relatively low, and the shadow of saxophonist Lester Young (or at least part of him) hovered over much of what they did.

FOUR

Jazz Deconstructed

Jazz can be totally improvised, and Jazz can be entirely composed before one note has been played. Jazz can be played in any time signature and on any instrument. The Jazz player has the option to play a composition precisely as it was written, or to submit it to the most radical changes.

One of the most puzzling things for someone seeing a Jazz group play for the first time is how do they all know what to play when there is no music on the bandstand? How do they know when to start and when to stop? Are they just making it all up off the top of their heads?

To many, composed music and improvised music seem to be opposites, but in Jazz, they merge in a unique fashion. It has been said that the best improvised music sounds composed, and that the best composed music sounds improvised.

Think about it: When you hear a great classical pianist play Chopin, or a superlative actor recite Shakespeare, they give the impression that they are actually inventing these ideas in front of you. In the same sense, a master improviser will occasionally hit upon a series of phrases that seem to have been preordained; you know where they are going, even though it is being created at the instant you are hearing it. The composer Arnold Schoenberg once wrote, "composition is slowed down improvisation," and both disciplines deal with the same challenge—how to organize and present ideas in a coherent fashion.

One of the most common misconceptions about Jazz is that it is spun out of the air in a totally impromptu manner. This notion came about because many small Jazz groups do not read music when they play. The truth of the matter is that those musicians are actually spontaneously creating a very sophisticated form of theme and variations. Imagine that you and a group of friends decided to do your own version of a favorite story—one that you know from a book or from a film, say, *The Wizard of Oz*. You decide who is going to play whom. It is understood that Dorothy is going to start in Kansas, there's going to be a tornado, she's going to encounter a gaggle of crazy characters in the land of Oz, and by the end, she will wake up in her own bed at home. The way that you get from scene to scene will be up to the actors at the moment, but they are all so familiar with the progression of events and the underlying theme/story that the improvisation adds a special kind of intensity and calls for a higher level of engagement. This frequently results in a new sense of excitement and the possibility of understanding this well-known story in a new fashion.

That, in essence, is what the players in a Jazz band do. They all know the tune beforehand, and the responsibilities of their chosen instruments. And even those indulging in free Jazz bring with them the experiences of how they usually do it, and this functions in that context as "the tune." The piano, guitar, bass, and drums have a dual role: They function as accompanists, providing the rhythmic and harmonic basis over which the other soloists will invent their own melodic variations, yet they also participate as soloists. The framework is flexible so that the soloists may shorten or lengthen their improvisations depending on the inspiration of the moment. The other players, then, have a responsibility to react to what has preceded them. Even when they are not soloing, members of a Jazz band have to be intimately attuned to the music at all times, because you never know what direction it might take. If you don't, you may, as John Coltrane once put it, feel as though you stepped into an empty elevator shaft. One way to follow a Jazz improvisation is to hear the melody of the song in your head while listening to the solo.

But improvisation is not the be all and end all of Jazz. Composers such as Duke Ellington and Eddie Sauter wrote some Jazz compositions that are practically devoid of improvisation. But the real challenge comes when a composer integrates improvisation into a piece. When playing orchestral Jazz compositions, the improviser has to use all of his or her faculties to weave a statement into the context that the composer created. This is why all Jazz musicians are composers.

Jazz improvisers may not sit down with pen in hand and write out their solos on a piece of score paper, but those solos nonetheless require the same discipline as the written works of a composer. One of the great pleasures to be found in listening to players who are both great composers and soloists, such as Benny Carter and Wynton Marsalis, is hearing them improvise on their own material. And if you ever have the chance to listen to a classic Jazz improvisation over and over again—Coleman Hawkins's "Body and Soul" or Thelonious Monk's "I Should Care," for example—you will find that they are compositions of the highest magnitude. Indeed, there is a good case to be made that these musicians should be able to copyright their solos as original compositions or variations.

Improvisation is a big part of everyday life. We improvise in the way we get dressed, cook our meals, go to work, and speak. There is no mystery to it, and there is certainly no mystery to Jazz improvisation. It is, simply put, just another way of spontaneously confronting a challenge. To hear the purest and most sublime example of Jazz improvisation, listen to Louis Armstrong. As the writer Stanley Crouch has observed, "In Armstrong's work there is a new kind of confidence that had never existed in Western music, an aural proof that man can master time through improvisation, that contemplation and action needn't be at odds." Armstrong's lessons still reverberate at the core of the music.

Up through the 1940s, the materials that Jazz players used were very close to those found in popular music. There was much in common between the composers of Broadway, film, and Tin Pan Alley, and the handful of original composers in Jazz. Indeed, in many cases, they aspired to success in both genres. Jerome Kern, Irving Berlin, George Gershwin, Harold Arlen, Richard Rodgers and others had been listening closely to the music that had been pouring out of the African-American community, and used it with great skill in their own creations. Jazz composers such as Jelly Roll Morton, Duke Ellington, and the other composers who wrote what we now call "Jazz" also drew out of that same musical well. The difference was that they were using Jazz's improvisatory essence as a major component of their styles. They also used the best Jazz musicians at their disposal to interpret their music, and encouraged them to make their own interpretations in the course of performance. Finally, they were open enough to incorporate the best of these interpretations into their written scores. So what we see in Jazz is a dialogue between the composer and the performer.

At its best, Jazz shares with other genres an innate form that flows out of its content. This may seem like an odd comment since a great deal of Jazz played today remains variations on a preset theme or structure that rarely varies during the performance. But there can be new forms within the solos themselves, or between the solos, that give the performance an ebb and flow that makes for an effective contrast with the regularity of the outer shell.

While rhythm is the primary component that defines Jazz, many will hear a Jazz piece and react to the "jazziness" of the melody, which often reflects the influence of the blues. Today, it can just as readily apply to a musical theme, with precious little reference to the melodic shapes that spawned Jazz almost a century ago. Basically, Jazz players today are doing the same thing Jazz players were doing back in the 1920s—creating variations on a theme and trying to swing.

"Swing" is a subjective term, to be sure. Any music that has a characteristically rhythmic lilt to it swings, whether it be African drum music, a Viennese waltz, or the work of J. S. Bach. The Jazz meaning of "swing" once again derives from Armstrong, and in his case it means that he felt free to play with the basic rhythm—surging ahead or lagging behind, but always knowing exactly where he was and always landing back on the beat at the crucial moment. This is the true meaning of the term rubato, and it is that rhythmic freedom that permits swing to occur. African music is intensely polyrhythmic, which means that different rhythmic patterns occur simultaneously— or at least that is the closest way we in the West can come to express what they are doing. This simultaneity survived the passage to slavery, and then later found expression in the African-American churches. That is why musicians such as Dizzy Gillespie, Milt Jackson, Wynton Marsalis, and many others have always given credit to church music as the real root of swing in Jazz.

If you really want to unlock the mysteries of Jazz, here is a good suggestion: Go find Louis Armstrong's recording of "Potato Head Blues." Listen for the trumpet solo that follows the clarinet solo and listen to it over and over again. When you feel that you really know it, sing along with the record. When you internalize the rhythm and the shapes of those trumpet phrases, you will have come as close to an understanding of the essence of Jazz as you are ever likely to need.

FIVE

The Musicians

Once one gets past the dozen or so incontrovertible innovators, it becomes nigh well impossible to set a rational limit on how many entries to include in a chapter such as this. No matter where it ends, there will always be people left out who seem to "trump" others who made the final cut. Where, one might ask, are Cannonball Adderley, Dave Brubeck, Billy Strayhorn, Buddy Rich, and Ray Brown, not to mention Tom Harrell, Woody Shaw, Lionel Hampton, Yusef Lateef, Gil Evans, and David Murray, or any number of younger lights such as Bill Charlap, Ken Peplowski, Peter Washington, Ralph Petersen, Jr., Jason Lindner, Django Bates, Mark Turner, and Kurt Rosenwinkel? There is no completely satisfactory answer. Here, however, the net has been cast as far and wide as possible to represent the widest spectrum of important players. The list even includes a handful of Jazz's definitive vocalists.

It should be noted that there is no connection between the relative significance of these innovators and the size of their biographies. Sometimes it just happens to be easier to capture the essence of a giant in fewer words than it is to introduce someone less familiar who made a less vital contribution. All of this is to say that in terms of these biographical segments, size doesn't matter.

Muhal Richard Abrams (b. 1930): A pianist/composer who came up in the fertile Chicago Jazz scene from the late 1950s on, playing with many of the top players and having his compositions recorded by Max Roach and others. Abrams took a giant leap in redefining the music and its presentation in the 1960s through his participation in the founding of the AACM. Through an eclectic mix of influences and presentations that brought back the theatricality that had been so much a part of Jazz's early heritage, the AACM and the groups it spawned, most notably the Art Ensemble of Chicago, enjoyed tremendous popularity during the '70s and early '80s. Anthony Braxton, among the players who came out of this heady atmosphere, appears on one of Abrams's classic recordings, the 1967 *Levels and Degrees of Light*. After relocating to New York in the 1970s, Abrams has composed prolifically for symphony orchestras, string quartets, solo piano, voice, and big bands in addition to making a series of larger ensemble recordings (*One Line, Two Views*) that include harp and accordion.

Louis Armstrong (1901–1971): The trumpeter/vocalist who remains the touchstone against which all Jazz music may be measured. Growing up in poverty in New Orleans during the musically fertile years leading up to World War I, Armstrong soaked up music wherever he could. He received cornet lessons during a short stint in a juvenile home, and by the time he left the Crescent City in 1923 to join his mentor, King Oliver, and his band in Chicago, Armstrong had arrived at a concept that was to radically alter the music for the remainder of the century. There was something so human and so noble in the sound of both his trumpet and his voice that it captivated listeners from every walk of life. Armstrong made classic recordings as a sideman throughout the '20s, with Oliver ("Tears"), with Fletcher Henderson's band ("T.N.T."), and with Bessie Smith ("St. Louis Blues"). But the recordings that taught the world precisely what Jazz was and pointed the way for what it would become were his Hot Fives and Sevens sessions of 1925–28. "West End Blues," "Weatherbird," "Basin Street Blues," and dozens of others caught an American equivalent of a Shakespeare or a Picasso in the white heat of creation and exerted an influence that remains vital to this day. It was only a matter of time until his message had spread to the entertainment world at large. Armstrong distinguished himself on Broadway, in films and radio, and in appearances around the world. By the late '30s, he had changed the way virtually every musician and singer of note understood American music. Armstrong led a big band from 1932–46, making classic recordings each and every year ("That's My Home," "Struttin' with Some Barbecue," "Swing that Music," "Sleepy Time Down South"), and then formed a sextet known as the All Stars, with which he played for the rest of his life. The U.S. State Department frequently sent Armstrong to troubled areas as an "Ambassador of Goodwill," where he reached the people in a way no diplomat could. The 1955 film *Satchmo the Great* captures many moments from this period of his career. He even managed to stem the rise of the Beatles, if only for a moment, when his recording of "Hello, Dolly" topped the charts in 1964. Dismissed by many at the time as a relic, it is now clear that Armstrong's art continued to mature. One of his trumpet notes could contain a greater emotional wallop than any number of big bands could muster. With the 1986 resurgence of his "What a Wonderful World," Armstrong had another number-one hit, this time posthumously. It proved once again that his way of shifting an accent here, or bending a note there—all infused with an irresistible joie de vivre—could still light up even the darkest day. It still can.

Count Basie (1904–84): One of the most original Jazz piano stylists and the leader of swinging big bands for over forty years. Although he was born in Red Bank, New Jersey, Basie (given name, William) found his own voice in the swinging sounds of late '20s Kansas City. After mastering the virtuosic stride piano style while a member of the Walter Page and Bennie Moten bands (Moten's *Prince of Wails*), Basie began to pare his playing down to the essentials. He pioneered the use of space in both solo and accompaniment, which made him the ideal pianist for his band's greatest soloist, tenor saxophonist Lester Young, who shared the same aesthetic preoccupations (*Jive at Five, Doggin' Around, Taxi War Dance*). The Basie band of the 1930s and 1940s maintained the feeling of a small group, with an emphasis on solos and on the rhythm section.

It was this informal air that lent the band an air of distinction in comparison with the more "organized" bands of the period. It would be hard to overestimate the influence this band had on the Jazz world at the time. Virtually every big band (and not just the hard-hitting Jazz ones) picked up on some aspect of Basie's soloists, ensemble phrasing, and rhythm section. After a brief spell leading an octet in the early '50s, Basie regrouped with a new band that was far more conventional than his earlier ones, but whose sheer strength and consistency earned it the nickname "The Swing Machine." Vocalist Joe Williams had a great success with the band in the '50s (*Everyday I Have the Blues*), and it remained one of the very few Jazz big bands to survive through the 1980s. Basie made a series of informal small-group recordings in the 1970s (some with pianist Oscar Peterson) that gave him a creative outlet he lacked in his own band. These sessions contain glimpses of his at once profound and risk-taking musicianship.

Sidney Bechet (1897–1959): A true titan of Jazz whose influence and fame may very well have been far greater if he had not been eclipsed by the force of nature that was Louis Armstrong, Bechet mastered the clarinet and soprano saxophone in his native New Orleans and played with an intensity that was truly mesmerizing. His appearances, in the States and in Europe in the late teens and early twenties, were transformative experiences for musicians as diverse as the Swiss conductor Ernest Ansermet and Duke Ellington. Bechet could create endless variations on any given chord progression, and these in turn became the basis of more variations, making him truly one of the first great Jazz composers. Both burdened and blessed with an insatiable appetite for music and for the high life, Bechet had run-ins with the law all over the globe before settling down to a relatively quiet existence in New York in the early '30s. After making a classic 1932 session with his New Orleans Feetwarmers (*Maple Leaf Rag* and *Shag*), Bechet worked with Noble Sissle's band for several years. He eventually found work hard to come by and opened a tailor shop. He set down a series of classic recordings for Victor in the early '40s in collaboration with the likes of Earl Hines ("Blues in Thirds"), Henry Red Allen ("Egyptian Fantasy"), Willie "The Lion" Smith ("I'm Coming Virginia"), and Big Sid Catlett ("Old Man Blues"). It wasn't until the revival of New Orleans Jazz in the mid-forties that Bechet got the attention he deserved, and he eventually expatriated to France, where he attained the status of a true icon.

Bix Beiderbecke (1903–31): This lyrical cornetist, pianist, and composer remains one of the most misunderstood figures in Jazz history. What is beyond dispute is that he created a melodic language all his own that had a profound impact on the music's development. Artists as diverse as Benny Goodman, Lester Young, Rex Stewart, and Benny Carter all played with a marked Beiderbecke influence at times. In addition, many arrangers, including Bill Challis, were influenced by his patterns of melodic construction. His 1927 small-group recordings of "I'm Coming Virginia" and "Singin' the Blues" (recorded under the leadership of his musical partner, Frankie Trumbauer) created a new approach to ballad playing. Beiderbecke had a bell-like tone on the cornet and an expressively vocal way of playing that was instantly recognizable. There was also a reflective air about his music. Raised in Iowa, he heard the Original Dixieland Jazz Band on record and Louis Armstrong in person (playing on a riverboat). Beiderbecke merged these influences with a marked predilection for the "light classical" music of the day, most of which was watered down Debussy and Ravel. His most famous composition, "In a Mist," is an original mixture of the blues and what was then thought of as "modernistic" harmony. Beiderbecke was featured in two of the greatest bands of his time, Jean Goldkette's and Paul Whiteman's, and made many classic recordings with them ("Clementine," "Lonely Melody," and "From Monday On"). From a sociological standpoint, Beiderbecke set the pattern for the alienated white youth who finds his artistic salvation in the music of black culture, but who cannot escape a self-destructive impulse that leads to an early, tragic death.

Art Blakey (1919–90): One of Jazz's most original and forceful drummers, and a bandleader who over the course of four decades brought many young musicians to prominence who later became important movers and shakers in their own rights, Blakey had a long association with Thelonious Monk and played on many of the pianist's greatest recordings. His style was far more elemental than those of Max Roach or Kenny Clarke, who were the guiding lights of the era, yet he exerted a great influence with his fire and drive. After a few years with the big bands of Fletcher Henderson and Billy Eckstine, Blakey formed his own group known as the Jazz Messengers. Originally a big band, it was pared down to a quintet co-led with pianist Horace Silver (A *Night at Bird-*

land). Sensing that Jazz was becoming too precious and losing its popularity in the early 1950s, Blakey set out to recapture a large audience with bands that swung hard and that played tunes that were meant to be just as inclusive as so much of modern Jazz had become exclusive; this became known as "hard bop." Silver left to form his own group in 1955 and Blakey became one of the very few successful drummer/bandleaders in Jazz. His group always showcased young talent and played their original compositions. Some of the most outstanding units had featured Lee Morgan, Benny Golson, and Bobby Timmons (*Moanin'*); Freddie Hubbard, Wayne Shorter, Curtis Fuller, and Cedar Walton (*Mosaic*); Woody Shaw, Carter Jefferson, and Steve Turre (*Anthenagin*); and Wynton Marsalis, Brandford Marsalis, Bill Pierce, and Donald Brown (*Keystone 3*). Many other great players also passed through Blakey's bands, all of whom received much encouragement and a trial by fire every night on the bandstand.

Jimmy Blanton (1918–42): During his short tenure in Duke Ellington's band, Blanton (who signed his name Jimmie) single-handedly brought the bass into the forefront of Jazz expression. All of the great bassists who preceded him were masters of accompaniment, but far from distinguished soloists. Blanton's radically advanced technique and the creative freedom he was given by Ellington gave him the opportunity to create a new identity for the instrument. In the course of one piece, Blanton ranged from solos to backgrounds and all the interesting areas in between, where he was at once supporting the band and also commenting on it. His feature with the band, "Jack the Bear," was imitated by bassists around the world. Ellington also recorded several classic duets with Blanton, including "Pitter Panther Patter" and "Mr. J. B. Blues." One can only imagine what Blanton may have accomplished if he had lived longer. A weak constitution and a penchant for all-night jam sessions made him susceptible to tuberculosis. He is one of the very few players on any instrument who influenced everyone who followed him for decades.

Clifford Brown (1930–56): A prodigious improviser and virtuoso whose early death in a car crash robbed Jazz of a vital influence, Brown rose to prominence in the early 1950s at a time when many of the music's brightest lights were being snuffed out by heroin addiction. Indeed, his mentor, trumpeter Fats Navarro, who blended a robust tone with startling velocity, died in 1950 of tuberculosis exacerbated by his addiction. Brown played with a brilliant sound and with a clarity of execution at the fastest tempos, but never sacrificed quality for quantity of notes. Even at his most fleet, every note meant something. Brown was a family man whose dedication to the clean life was a great inspiration to his peers. He played in various bands, including those of Lionel Hampton and Tadd Dameron (*A Study in Dameronia*) before pairing up with the great Jazz drummer Max Roach as coleader of a quintet. Their repertoire was challenging, and they quickly became one of Jazz's most popular attractions. Luckily, Brown recorded prolifically with Roach ("Joy Spring," "Jordu," and "Parisian Thoroughfare"), and during his brief moment in the limelight also made classic sessions with Dinah Washington, Sarah

Vaughan, and a string section arranged by Neal Hefti (*Brownie: The Complete Emarcy Recordings of Clifford Brown*).

Benny Carter (b. 1907): A brilliant instrumentalist (alto saxophone, clarinet, trumpet, and others) and composer whose long life has paralleled the evolution of the music, Carter was one of the prime movers in the development of his main instrument, the alto saxophone, and in the creation of the modern Jazz orchestra, known as the big band. Carter played and wrote for the finest bands of the 1920s (Fletcher Henderson, McKinney's Cotton Pickers, Chick Webb) and developed an elegant sound that was widely influential. His trademark became his writing for the saxophone section, but that credit sometimes unfortunately masks his equal mastery of the other sections of the band. Carter recorded many classic big band pieces in 1933 ("Symphony in Riffs," "Blue Lou," and "Lonesome Nights") that introduced pianist Teddy Wilson to the Jazz world, but found sustained work hard to come by. By this point, Carter had become proficient on the clarinet and the trumpet, recording many classic solos on these and other instruments. At the same time, he became the main arranger for the Benny Goodman band, and it was his arrangements that led to the band's first successes. Unable to keep his own group going and frustrated at the limits placed upon him in the U.S., Carter spent three years in Europe (1935–38). He led interracial bands, made historic recordings with Django Reinhardt and Coleman Hawkins ("Crazy Rhythm" and "Honeysuckle Rose"), and was a featured arranger/player/composer with orchestras throughout the Continent. Of special note are the saxophone ensemble recordings he wrote and played on ("I'm Coming Virginia"). After returning home, Carter reformed his big band, and eventually settled in Los Angeles, where he was the first black composer to establish himself in the Hollywood studios. Carter also was a prolific writer of pop tunes, and had a World War II hit with "Cow Cow Boogie." He managed to keep a foot in the Jazz world, touring with Jazz at the Philharmonic and recording elegant and timeless albums (*Jazz Giant* and *Further Definitions*), including a 1952 studio jam session with Charlie Parker and Johnny Hodges. Carter resumed a full schedule of playing and touring in the mid-seventies and has since received virtually every honor imaginable around the world and continues to compose and arrange. During the '80s and '90s he recorded a series of extended compositions, including "Central City Sketches," "Harlem Renaissance," and "Tales of the Rising Sun."

Sid Catlett (1910–51): A great drummer who possessed a rare combination of showmanship and artistry that made him a favorite among musicians and the public. His understanding of the nature of Jazz rhythm was such that he could play with musicians of any stylistic bent and fit like a glove. Catlett grew up in and around Chicago, where he got to hear the New Orleans master drummers Baby Dodds and Zutty Singleton, who were major contributors to the burgeoning idiom. He was also enamored of the many "show" drummers of the day, and found a way to combine these influences into an artistic whole. Catlett played with many top big bands— Benny Carter, Don Redman, and Benny Goodman—but his longest and most significant association was with Louis Armstrong, who named Catlett as his favorite drummer. His playing on the 1947 album *Satchmo at Symphony Hall* is some of the best Jazz drumming ever recorded. From a basic Jazz drum set, Catlett produced a panoply of sounds that would be the envy of a large orchestra's entire percussion section; plus, he swung. During his periods away from Armstrong, Catlett led his own small bands on 52nd Street, and made many classic recording sessions, most notably with James P. Johnson ("After You've Gone"), Lester Young ("Afternoon of a Basie-ite"), and Charlie Parker/Dizzy Gillespie ("Salt Peanuts").

Charlie Christian (1916–42): Like the bassist Jimmy Blanton, guitarist Christian's recorded career spans only a couple of years, but his influence is still felt today. A product of the Southwest, Christian was one of the first disciples of the tenor saxophonist Lester Young. After playing various instruments, including the bass, Christian settled on the electric guitar and was tutored by Eddie Durham, who had been among the first to introduce the instrument through his work with Bennie Moten, Jimmie Lunceford, and Count Basie. In 1939, the pianist Mary Lou Williams told talent scout John Hammond about Christian, who in turn arranged an audition with Benny Goodman. Within weeks, Christian was featured in a new Goodman small group, the Sextet, and also on occasion with the big band. His playing took its cue from Young's even phrasing and penchant for long melodic lines. Christian had an inexhaustible imagination and structured his solos with care ("Seven Come Eleven," "Stardust," and "Air Mail Special"). When the Goodman band was in New York, Christian would go to Harlem after work to jam with young musicians such as Dizzy Gillespie, Thelonious Monk, and Kenny Clarke. Luckily, a handful of these sessions were recorded, and they are an invaluable documentation of a vital part of Christian's abilities that was never captured on the Goodman recordings (*Swing to Bop*). He plays extended solos that are teeming with new ideas, many of which were of great inspiration not only to virtually every guitarist that followed in his wake, but also to Monk and Lennie Tristano. The late-night hours and a weak constitution led to tuberculosis and an early death.

Nat "King" Cole (1919–65): Better known for his smooth voice and charming personality, Cole was also one of the most original Jazz pianists. As a singer, he did not have the rhythmic vitality of an Armstrong, a Holiday, or a Sinatra, but at the piano he was a true dynamo. Cole heard pianist Earl Hines in his native Chicago as a teenager and gleaned much from the master's spikily dissonant and hard-swinging style. Later on, he also listened closely to Count Basie, Teddy Wilson, and Art Tatum; it is a testament to his originality that these influences never overwhelmed him. After touring with a show, Cole formed his trio in 1938, and its instrumentation and style set the standard for such groups (piano, guitar, bass) that continues to this day. Smart arrangements, slick performances, and novelty tunes ("Straighten Up and Fly Right") were what captivated the public, but musicians were also aware of Cole's capacity for tremendous invention and relaxed vocal phrasing ("Sweet Lorraine"). As his star rose (eventually making Cole a household name), the piano took more and more of a back-seat to his singing. Luckily, Cole recorded prolifically throughout his early years and there are literally hundreds of outstanding trio performances. Cole was also a master at accompanying horn players. Of special significance are the titles he recorded in tandem with Lester Young ("Tea for Two," "Body and Soul," "Back to the Land," and "I Want to Be Happy"). Marked by their intensity and understatement, these sessions (two done in the studio and one live radio date) are highlights of both of their careers.

Ornette Coleman (b. 1930): Alto saxophonist and composer whose music, known reductively as "free Jazz," was as elemental as it was experimental. By the late 1950s, many musicians felt trapped by Jazz's harmonic and formal conventions. Ornette Coleman ultimately made the biggest break with the Jazz tradition. After playing with blues and Jazz bands in his native Texas, Coleman moved to Los Angeles, where his radical approach made him a notorious figure. Pianist-composers Paul Bley and John Lewis, and composer Gunther Schuller—founders of third-stream music—heard a fresh and blues-rooted voice in Coleman's music, and championed his cause, which resulted in a recording contract and an engagement in New York's Five Spot in 1959. Although his music remained controversial (*Change of the Century* and *Free Jazz*), it exerted an enormous influence on Sonny Rollins and John Coltrane. At its best, Coleman's music was based on a series of melodic variations that knew no harmonic boundaries. His bands featured like-minded players such as cornetists Don Cherry and Bobby Bradford, saxophonist Dewey Redman, bassists Charlie Haden and David Izenson, and drummers Ed Blackwell and

Charles Moffett. Coleman has attempted to play other instruments, including the violin and trumpet, but it is his saxophone playing that remains definitive. Coleman tried his hand at orchestra music ("Skies over America") with mixed results and in recent decades delved into the world of Jazz-rock and fusion in a typically idiosyncratic fashion with his band Prime Time. In the mid-nineties, Coleman recorded with a pianist (Geri Allen) for the first time in decades, and the two albums that resulted (*Three Women* and *Hidden Man*) may very well attain the status of classics in his already large discography.

John Coltrane (1926–67): Perhaps no other figure in the music made as great a progression over the course of his career as did saxophonist Coltrane. As a young man, he played alto saxophone in the Charlie Parker mold, and then switched to the tenor where he showed a marked Dexter Gordon influence. Although Miles Davis and Dizzy Gillespie took note of his individuality in the early 50s, Coltrane stumbled through the first half of that decade. He was in and out of Davis's quintet in 1955–56 before experiencing a spiritual revival while a member of Thelonious Monk's quartet. From that moment on there was no holding him back. Coltrane rejoined Davis for another couple of years before becoming a leader in his own right. A series of challenging albums containing many of his own original compositions, beginning with *Giant Steps*, established him as a Jazz innovator of the first rank. Coltrane's 1960 reworking of "My Favorite Things" (from *The Sound of Music*) became an unexpected Jazz hit and catapulted him into a major international attraction. Unlike most musicians fortunate enough to tickle the public's fancy while remaining true to their muse, Coltrane's protean nature kept his music evolving. One project involved brass and woodwinds (*The Africa Brass Sessions*), while there also were more reflective collaborations with Duke Ellington and vocalist Johnny Hartman. Coltrane's original music became more involved, and on many pieces, pianist McCoy Tyner and bassist Jimmy Garrison eventually gave way to extended duets between Coltrane and drummer Elvin Jones. Always a vocal player, Coltrane worked on a series of saxophone techniques that combined tremendous velocity with a cry that was unsettling to some and beautiful to others. Coltrane's music had a unique spirituality to it ("A Love Supreme" and "Crescent") and by the end of his life he was addressing his thoughts about the cosmos accompanied by bells and other percussion. His influence remains a vital one more than three decades after his death.

Chick Corea (b. 1941): A distinctive composer, pianist, and bandleader who thrived by straddling various styles and approaches to music over the course of his long career. During the early to mid-sixties, Corea played with Mongo Santamaria, Willie Bobo (1962–63), and Blue Mitchell (1964–66), and this mixture of Jazz and Latin musics set a pattern for the rest of his career. Corea established himself as a new voice in the heady world of Jazz piano in the mid-sixties with a series of trio albums (*Tones for Joan's Bones, Now He Sings,* and *Now He Sobs*). They reflected the primary influences of the day, but were distinguished by his fresh compositions and a tangibly exploratory feeling. His two years with Miles Davis (1968–70) brought him international exposure, and Corea contributed strongly to the trumpeter's juxtapositions of free Jazz styles with the use of electronic instruments and rock/funk rhythms. Feeling a desire to return to an acoustic setting, Corea formed a quartet, Circle (that included Anthony Braxton and Dave Holland), and also recorded a series of solo piano albums. This was followed by a sudden immersion into the world of electronics and fusion music with the group Return to Forever, which in its different incarnations varied between rock, fusion, Latin, and Jazz. It was also during the '70s that Corea's tunes ("Spain" and "La Fiesta") became parts of the standard contemporary repertoire. From that time on, Corea has led his Elektric and Akoustic bands, tributes to Bud Powell and Thelonious Monk, played classical music, and in general, been extraordinarily engaged in keeping his music, no matter what the mode, contemporary. His band Origin featured some of the outstanding young players of the '90s, including saxophonist Steve Wilson and bassist Avishai Cohen.

Miles Davis (1926–91): One of the most immediately recognizable Jazz trumpet stylists and a consummate bandleader who knew how to turn a unit into more than the sum of its individual parts. Raised in middle-class comfort in St. Louis, Davis experienced an epiphany (which he claimed, later in life, had never been equaled) in 1944 when he heard Charlie Parker and Dizzy Gillespie—passing through his hometown with Billy Eckstine's band—for the first time. In less than a year, Davis was in New York being mentored by those two and the likes of Coleman Hawkins and Thelonious Monk. Listening to his first recordings with Parker and Hawkins, it is far from readily apparent that Davis was a talent worth nurturing. He benefited greatly from the high-level contexts he played in, and a decade later would offer the same help up the ladder to others whose potential was hard to spot, such as John Coltrane. His first recordings as a leader, using most of the Parker Quintet with which he was then working—but with Parker switching to the tenor saxophone—were made in 1947 (*Half Nelson, Milestones*). The mood is more reflective and the sound somehow deeper than most contemporary Jazz, revealing that Davis already knew how to realize his budding musical persona. Davis's trumpet technique grew by leaps and bounds during his years in Parker's quintet (1945–48), and by the time he formed his first band in late 1948, he had become a major stylist. Both his playing and his Nonet were strong reactions against the prolixity and formlessness of much of the bop music of the era. Davis was inspired by the use of tuba and woodwinds and the general elegance of the Claude Thornhill band, and all of his arrangers—Gil Evans ("Moon Dreams"), Gerry Mulligan ("Jeru"), John Carisi ("Israel"), and John Lewis ("Rouge")—placed a priority on the use of space and of a greatly expanded tonal and dynamic range. Though the band has attained great historical status, it was a commercial bust and ushered in a period of five years during which Davis made a handful of wonderful recordings ("Dear Old Stockholm," "Bag's Groove," and "The Man I Love") but spent the great majority of his time battling drug addiction. He emerged in 1955 with a breakthrough appearance at the Newport Jazz Festival, leading to a contract with a major label that enabled Davis to realize his ambitious artistic visions. These included orchestral projects with Evans (*Miles Ahead, Sketches of Spain,* and *Porgy and Bess*) and small-group recordings that set the musical fashions for years to come (*Milestones, Kind of Blue, Miles Ahead,* and *In a Silent Way*). John Coltrane, Bill Evans, Cannonball Adderley, Herbie Hancock, Wayne Shorter, Chick Corea, and Tony Williams all grew exponentially as artists during their time with Davis's quintet, and the exposure they gained made it possible for them to then branch out as leaders in their own rights. Davis confronted every development in Jazz through the late '60s in his own rigorously personal fashion. At the end of that decade, he made an abrupt shift in musical style and began an effort to woo the young audiences that had deserted Jazz for rock and funk music. Musicians such as Jimi Hendrix and Sly and the family Stone became Davis's inspiration, all of this reflected in a series of albums beginning with *Bitches Brew, Live/Evil,* and *Jack Johnson*. Davis, for decades a charismatic leader of Jazz styles, attracted many Jazz musicians into the tricky waters of fusion music. Davis continued to chase the trends of popular music, including some of the seamier sides of rap, for the rest of his life. Many top players passed through these later Davis bands, including Kenny Garrett, Foley, Marcus Miller, and Al Foster. Just months before his death, Davis revisited his classic collaborations with Gil Evans. Although health problems forced him to deputize the young trumpeter Wallace Roney to cover most of his original parts, Davis revealed that he had retained the majesty and sophistication of his acoustic years by playing a handful of heartbreakingly fragile, yet dense solos.

Eric Dolphy (1928–64): A virtuoso on the flute, bass clarinet, and alto saxophone who always pushed the boundaries of what was deemed to be acceptable in Jazz. Today, his playing sounds daring, but certainly within the confines of what we call Jazz. In the early '60s, however, Dolphy incited many reputable musicians and critics to label his music (and that of his colleague John Coltrane) "anti-Jazz." The incorporation of eccentric sounds into Jazz has a tradition that goes back to New Orleans, but by Dolphy's time, there were political and social agendas within the Jazz world that were clashing, and it was the musicians who paid the price. Dolphy came up in the musical mainstream of Los Angeles in the 1950s, and had mastered the music of Charlie Parker before he began experimenting with notes and sounds that many found unsettling. He received much exposure through his work with drummer Chico Hamilton's band in the late '50s. Dolphy's years in New York were marked by a high profile in the Jazz press (much of it controversial, but he was taken very seriously) and a steady diminution of actual work. There were recordings and engagements with Charles Mingus, including sessions with Roy Eldridge and Bud Powell, in addition to both small and large Mingus bands, John Lewis's Orchestra U.S.A., and a quintet he co-led with trumpeter Booker Little. Their 1961 *Live! At the Five Spot* quickly became a classic. Dolphy attached himself to the Coltrane Quartet for a short period in 1961–62, and even toured Europe with them for no fee. Dolphy found his greatest outlet in a series of recordings under his own name that reflected his original and sometimes humorous conception; his final album *Out to Lunch* is definitive. There was also a European tour with Charles Mingus in 1964 that resulted in several live albums that find Dolphy at the top of his game.

Dave Douglas (b. 1963): One of the major trumpet stylists and composers in contemporary Jazz, Douglas frequently cites his major influences as Igor Stravinsky, John Coltrane, and Stevie Wonder. That sort of eclecticism is not nearly as unusual in today's world as it might have been in the past. What is worthy of note is that Douglas has managed to construct a coherent musical vision of these diverse inspirations, and has, most surprisingly, created a substantial following both within and without the Jazz world. Douglas is committed to breaking down the barriers that exist between Jazz and other genres, but his music retains a Jazz profile by virtue of his trumpet playing, which seems comfortable in virtually every style. Douglas played with Horace Silver in the late '80s, and began recording his own albums in the early '90s with several different ensembles. One notable session with the Tiny Bell Trio reflected a Balkan influence ("Constellations"). Recent highlights include a tribute to Mary Lou Williams ("Soul on Soul"), which is about as close as Douglas has gotten on disc to Jazz's older traditions, and a quartet that includes the accordionist Guy Klucevsek and the versatile bassist Greg Cohen ("A Thousand Evenings").

Roy Eldridge (1911–89): One of the most impassioned and influential trumpeters in Jazz, Eldridge's diminutive stature, offset by his tremendous authority, earned him the nickname "Little Jazz." Inspired early on by the flowing, long-lined improvisations of tenor saxophonist Coleman Hawkins, Eldridge developed a virtuosic style that was harmonically advanced. After several years touring in territory bands, he established himself in New York and Chicago in the mid-thirties as a featured soloist with the big bands of Teddy Hill and Fletcher Henderson (alongside his close friend tenor saxophonist Chu Berry) before organizing his own group. His influence spread via a spate of recorded solos made with Gene Krupa, Teddy Wilson, Mildred Bailey, and Billie Holiday before he began to record under his own name ("After You've Gone" and "Wabash Stomp"). Unable to get his own band off the ground, he joined Gene Krupa in 1941 and was heavily featured as both trumpeter and vocalist and several hit recordings followed. Two of the best are "Let Me Off Uptown" and "Rockin' Chair." Eldridge had better luck with his own big band thereafter, but eventually led small groups, including a quintet with Coleman Hawkins ("At the Opera House") from the mid-fifties through the mid-sixties. Producer Norman Granz made Eldridge a regular member of his Jazz at the Philharmonic troupe beginning in the late '40s, and this led to years of international touring and high-profile recording. One 1949 concert found him in exceptional form playing alongside Charlie Parker and Lester Young ("Embraceable You"). In later years, Eldridge led the house band at New York's Jimmy Ryan's, and after a heart ailment forced him to stop playing in the mid-eighties, he continued to appear as a singer and never lost the electricity that defined his work.

Duke Ellington (1899–1974): There has never been a greater American composer than this Washington, D.C., native who led his own orchestra for almost five decades. As a student of the important African-American composers Will Marion Cook and Will Vodery, Ellington (born Edward Kennedy Ellington) was obsessed from an early age with creating a music that reflected his own heritage and was not a pale imitation of European conventions. Ellington was also an original piano stylist who transposed what he learned from his mentors James P. Johnson and Willie "The Lion" Smith to his own idiosyncratic ends. After coming to New York with a vaudeville band, Ellington formed a small Jazz band that created a sensation. This led to recordings and eventually to an engagement at Harlem's Cotton Club. Out of this came more recordings, national radio broadcasts, and film appearances. When that association came to an end in the late '30s, Ellington and band continued to tour the world (in later years as a representative of the U.S. State Department) and crisscrossed the United States innumerable times, playing dance dates, concerts, and everything in between. Ellington was one of those rare artists who wrote music that appealed to both the masses and those interested in fine art. Throughout the '30s and '40s, he had many hit songs ("Mood Indigo," "Solitude," "I Got It Bad," "Do Nothin' Till You Hear from Me," and "Sophisticated Lady") while at the same time composing extended pieces whose home was outside of the ballroom ("Reminiscing in Tempo," "Black," and "Brown and Beige"). A signal achievement of Ellington's was that there was no difference in the artistic quality between these pieces. Ellington never wrote up or down to his audiences—he was a straight shooter in this regard. During the '50s and '60s, Ellington (and his writing companion, Billy Strayhorn) created a number of suites, including *Such Sweet Thunder, A Drum*

Is a Woman, and *The Far East Suite* in addition to a superlative adaptation of themes from *The Nutcracker* and *Peer Gynt Suite.* Dozens of superlative players peopled the Ellington band: It was not unusual for some to stay for over a decade. The baritone saxophonist Harry Carney, whose cavernous sound and versatility was a bedrock of the band, joined in 1926 and remained there until Ellington's death. As a pianist, Ellington was startlingly original and had a profound influence on Thelonious Monk. In the 1960s, he played in small-group sessions with John Coltrane, Louis Armstrong, Coleman Hawkins, Charles Mingus, and Max Roach that remain classic examples of Jazz piano individuality. It was also during his final decade that he composed his *Sacred Concerts,* a mixed bag that nonetheless contains some of his best late melodies.

Bill Evans (1929–80): An understated, lyrical musician whose approach redefined Jazz piano in the 1960s, Evans brought a meditative approach to the piano trio that made for a great contrast with the prevailing fashions of the day. He came to prominence through his late '50s recordings with George Russell ("All About Rosie") and Miles Davis ("Kind of Blue"). Indeed, Davis went out of his way to say how much inspiration he got from Evans's fresh approach to Jazz piano. Evans's own trio featured a three-way dialogue with bassist Scott LaFaro and drummer Paul Motian that was a radical departure from the norm. One of their classic recordings is "Sunday at the Village Vanguard." Like Thelonious Monk, Evans never simply "jammed" a tune. Each song in his group's repertoire had an arrangement and was tightly moored to the specific melodic, harmonic, and rhythmic profile of the piece at hand. Evans also thrived in the recording studio working on special projects. His overdubbed "Conversations with Myself" and the duets with guitarist Jim Hall ("Undercurrent" and "Intermodulation") are highlights of his extensive recorded legacy. There was a continual development in Evans's playing right up to his death, and his last trio with bassist Marc Johnson and drummer Joe LaBarabera elicited some of Evans's strongest playing in years.

Ella Fitzgerald (1917–96): It was clear from the beginning of her career that Fitzgerald sang in a fashion that gave her great appeal both within and without the Jazz world. Her innate musicianship blended with the optimism in her voice to create an unbeatable combination. It was her vocal that made Chick Webb's 1938 recording of "A Tisket, A Tasket" one of the great commercial successes of the Swing Era. After Webb's untimely death a year later, Fitzgerald took over the band and never worked for anyone else again. Throughout the '40s, she had many hit recordings and was paired with many of the greatest entertainers of her time. Her 1946 duet with Louis Armstrong ("You Won't Be Satisfied Until You Break My Heart") is a perfect example of how she phrased abstractly like a Jazz horn without losing the immediacy the lyrics afforded. The 1950s saw her rise to a level of popularity that transcended Jazz, and she became an international icon. Her duets with pianist Ellis Larkins (*Pure Ella*), the *Songbook* series, and a handful of collaborations with Duke Ellington are among the highlights of her long recording career. Fitzgerald weathered the rock years better than most, and as her instrument gradually waned, she found herself plumbing greater emotional depths than she had earlier in her career.

Bill Frisell (b. 1951): Like Charlie Christian and Jim Hall, Frisell developed an original voice that related strongly to the electric guitar's legacy and at the same time pointed firmly in a new direction. Frisell was raised in Colorado, and then studied with Jim Hall and at the Berklee College of Music in Boston. The many years he spent as the house guitarist at ECM Records first established his reputation. His musical interests include Jazz, but are not limited to Jazz, and Frisell has recorded many albums that reflect his broad tastes. When he does choose to play Jazz, however, he can be brilliantly original. Drawing on a wide range of effects, including several adapted from Jimi Hendrix, Frisell uses distortion in a distinctly musical way. At the root of Frisell's art is a love of melody and a very sophisticated harmonic sense. His playing on the *Paul Motian on Broadway* series and in duet with pianist Fred Hersch (*Songs We Know*) may be the best introduction to his work in a Jazz context.

Kenny Garrett (b. 1960): For many years now, Garrett has been widely regarded as the outstanding alto saxophonist of his generation. Garrett was hired at a very young age by both Art Blakey and Miles Davis, experience which gave him an invaluable foundation. He was also featured early on by trumpet masters Freddie Hubbard and Woody Shaw. Garrett has developed steadily over the past decade, evolving an original sound and conception that is readily identifiable. His recordings have never been slipshod jam sessions, but are always carefully considered projects that reflect his outlook. Some have been tributes (*Pursuance: The Music of John Coltrane*) while others have dealt with programs that are exclusively contemporary (his own *Songbook*). But what they all have in common is Garrett's meticulous musicianship and dedication to spur-of-the-moment improvisation.

Stan Getz (1927–91): Few Jazz musicians have arrived at as immediately recognizable a sound as did tenor saxophonist Stan Getz. Breathy, intimate, and playful, Getz's playing would be unimaginable without the influence of Lester Young, but Getz had evolved into a distinct stylist by his twenty-fifth birthday. A supreme melodist and a superb technician, Getz began his career in the big bands of Jack Teagarden, Stan Kenton, and Benny Goodman before achieving fame with Woody Herman's Second Herd in 1947–49. His feature number, "Early Autumn," established his reputation as a ballad player, but his uptempo virtuosity ("Parker '51") would earn him the respect of his peers, including the young John Coltrane, who named Getz as one of his favorites. He spent a great part of the 1950s leading his own small groups (including a superb quintet with valve trombonist Bob Brookmeyer) and touring and recording for producer Norman Granz's Jazz at the Philharmonic troupe. Various personal and professional problems resulted in his expatriation to Scandinavia in the late '50s, where he continued to work with visiting American Jazzmen whenever possible. Shortly after returning home in 1961, he recorded two of his most classic albums. *Focus* was composed for him by Eddie Sauter and featured a string orchestra playing decidedly noncommercial compositions. *Jazz Samba* (made in tandem with the guitarist Charlie Byrd) launched the whole bossa nova craze, and the hit single from a subsequent album, *The Girl from Impanema*, would forever be associated with Getz. This bought him a commercial cachet that sustained the rest of his career. He dabbled in electronics and various contemporary trends, but always reverted to an acoustic Jazz setting. Getz's last recordings include an inspired duet with pianist Kenny Barron ("People Time").

Dizzy Gillespie (1917–93): Known for his upturned trumpet and billowing cheeks, Gillespie (born John Birks Gillespie) was a rare combination of music intellectual and showman. A relentless experimenter, he pushed the traditional boundaries of the trumpet to play fast more consistently than anyone who had preceded him. He also spent much of his playing time in the trumpet's upper register, and favored angular, dissonant phrases for effect. Years of playing in big bands (most notably with Teddy Hill and Cab Calloway) gave him a thorough grounding in Jazz composition, and he subsequently wrote many pieces that became popular ("A Night in Tunisia," "Salt Peanuts," and "Con Alma"). His collaborations with Charlie Parker in 1945 created the style Jazz would follow for decades. Gillespie was a natural teacher and literally showed generations of musicians (beginning with Max Roach, Miles Davis, and James Moody) how to play their instruments and about the specific musical theories that came to be known (reductively) as bop or bebop. His recordings from the 1940s ("I Can't Get Started" and "Things to Come") were studied around the world. Gillespie was one of the first Jazz musicians to integrate his music with Afro-Cuban influences ("Manteca"), and this led to a whole new genre. Indeed, in later years, Gillespie emphasized his international scope by hiring musicians from all around the world and eschewing his classic repertoire for music he found more current. Although he never lost his love for his big band, economics forced him to play with small groups for most of his career, and he structured their performances with an awareness of entertainment value, something he credited to his mentor Fats Waller. His reunions with his one-time idol Roy Eldridge in the '50s are superlative, as are some of the theme-oriented, small-group albums of the '60s (*Dizzy on the French Riviera*). In later years, an appearance on the children's show *The Muppets* gained him a new generation of fans.

Benny Goodman (1909–86): A superlative Jazz clarinetist and bandleader who had become a bona-fide cultural icon by his thirtieth birthday. He had few of the prerequisites for such fame with the exception of the sheer quality and magnetism of his music. Goodman played Jazz with an unprecedented technical facility wedded to a natural feeling for blues and swing. He also exerted influence in other arenas. His early championing of classical music, which included the commissioning and recording of a piece with and by Bela Bartok ("Contrasts"), broke down many barriers that separated Jazz from other genres of fine art. Born to immigrant parents in Chicago, Goodman showed a natural affinity for the clarinet. He worked professionally by his early teens and became the main breadwinner for his family. Goodman came to New York with Ben Pollack's band and became a fixture in the radio and recording studios by virtue of his reading and so-loing abilities. He made dozens of classic, small-group sessions throughout the late '20s and early '30s, and his work caught the ear of many of his contemporaries, including Lester Young. Goodman found his musical life wanting, however, and formed a big band in 1934 that after several starts and stops enjoyed a tremendous success in the fall of 1935. Their recordings sold well ("King Porter Stomp," and "Stompin' at the Savoy"); they appeared in films, on the radio, and in person all over the country. Goodman also heavily featured his small groups, which included pianist Teddy Wilson and vibra-phonist Lionel Hampton, and his racially integrated group broke down many walls in the entertainment industry. Their recordings remain some of the most original and timeless music of the era ("Who," "Body and Soul," and "Opus 1/2"). Goodman's fame peaked with his 1938 Carnegie Hall Concert. The band, which included Harry James and Gene Krupa, had reached a rarely achieved level of ensemble perfection. Featured artists included players from the Count Basie and Duke Ellington bands, and the recording, issued twelve years later, remains a Jazz best-seller. Although his repertoire ossified relatively early in his career, Goodman usually managed to find new variations on the familiar texts, and on occasion could still play in a fashion that showed him to be unsurpassed as an instrumentalist. This frequently happened when he had a great player in his own band, such as Charlie Christian, Mel Powell, Cootie Williams, or Ruby Braff. A 1962 Russian tour was an internationally covered event and marked one of the last artistic high points in his career. Goodman continued to alternate between classical music and Jazz until his death.

Jim Hall (b. 1930): The great majority of Jazz guitarists who appeared in the wake of Charlie Christian had a hard time getting beyond his tremendous influence. Even the earliest recorded examples of Jim Hall's playing from the mid-fifties reveal an original and quiet voice that rejected cliché and cant. He was an integral part of some of the finest small groups of the era, most notably those of Chico Hamilton and Jimmy Guiffre. But it was as a member of the Sonny Rollins Quartet in 1961–62 that Hall established himself as the premier voice on his instrument. Very few pianists or guitarists could have batted it back and forth as well as Hall did with as imposing an improviser as Rollins. Their album, *The Bridge*, is on virtually everyone's essential Jazz recordings list. Hall went from there to coleading a quartet with the lyrical flugelhornist Art Farmer (*Live at the Half Note*) and then to doing his own projects exclusively. Among the highlights are duets with Bill Evans and with bassist Ron Carter ("Alone Together"). As a young man, Hall studied classical composition and in recent years he has issued a series of orchestral recordings featuring his original compositions (*Dialogues, Textures*, and *By Arrangement*).

Herbie Hancock (b. 1940): Pianist and composer whose musical profile is so wide that he has Jazz fans who are ignorant of his pop music and vice-versa. Born in Chicago, Hancock was a child prodigy (he played a movement of a Mozart Piano Concerto with the Chicago Symphony Youth concert at the age of eleven) and graduated from Iowa's Grinnell College in 1960. Upon returning to his native Chicago, Hancock became a first-call Jazz pianist, playing with visiting giants like tenor saxophonist Coleman Hawkins and trumpeter Donald Byrd, the latter of whom was so impressed that in 1961 he invited Hancock to join his band in New York City. Hancock quickly became one of the most influential musicians of the era. Inspired by Wynton Kelly, Bill Evans, and the music of Ornette Coleman, among others, Hancock found his own subtle yet strong voice at the piano. In quick succession came the classic Blue Note albums, his tune "Watermelon Man" (recorded by over 200 artists), and an historic five years with Miles Davis. In tandem with bassist Ron Carter and drummer Tony Williams, Hancock created a new role for the Jazz rhythm section in which any element of the piece at hand could be radically altered. The three shared an almost-telepathic communication that could be truly shocking as they spontaneously changed forms, tempo, and mood. Hancock also contributed many pieces to the band's library, as did tenor saxophonist Wayne Shorter. Hancock's series of albums under his own name had their own smooth musical profile (*Empyrean Isles* and *Maiden Voyage*). Many of the pieces were modal in nature and gave the musicians a chance to expand their solos beyond just "playing the changes." After leaving Davis in 1969, Hancock's career as a leader took a few years to hit its stride. The tremendous success of The Headhunters in the early '70s was based on Hancock's incorporation of electric instruments and elements of rock, disco, and funk. He wrote innovative film scores (*Blowup* and *Deathwish*), and it was Hancock's strong desire to escape what he felt were the limitations of the Jazz audience that led to his 1983 MTV hit *Rockit*. There were patches of "straight-ahead" Jazz playing beginning in the late '70s, and in recent years Hancock has continued with acoustic efforts, including albums featuring duets with Wayne Shorter and Chick Corea, in addition to a tribute to George Gershwin.

Coleman Hawkins (1904–69): The creator of the idiom of the tenor saxophone in Jazz. Virtually every subsequent development in Jazz can be seen in relation to the series of events set in motion by Hawkins's unremitting dedication to being a true improviser. Never one to shy away from a musical challenge, Hawkins confronted the new music that he encountered over his long career and strove to integrate the parts he liked into his own conception. After playing the piano and the cello as a teen, Hawkins picked up the saxophone at a time when it was not taken seriously as an instrument. Played mostly for comic effects, few saw its potential beyond vaudeville. It wasn't until Hawkins encountered the young Louis Armstrong when they were both members of Fletcher Henderson's band in 1924–25 that he began to grow as an artist. Inspired by Armstrong's genius to find his own voice, Hawkins grew rapidly and by 1926 was creating solos that became studies for aspiring Jazz musicians ("The Chant"). He had a lifelong obsession with the music of Bach and was a great admirer of the cellist Pablo Casals, which is reflected in the intense yet singularly nonsentimental passion of his tenor saxophone improvisations. During his decade as the featured soloist with Henderson, Hawkins pioneered new approaches to both ballads ("It's the Talk of the Town" and "I've Got a Right to Sing a Torch Song") and rhythm tunes ("King Porter Stomp" and "Hocus Pocus"). By 1934, both Ellington and Armstrong had successfully toured Europe, and Hawkins, anxious for a change of scene, followed in their footsteps; but instead of returning home, he remained overseas for five years. He lived the high life, toured and recorded constantly, and experienced a lifestyle not possible in the United States. When he landed in New York in the summer of 1939, many thought that his days as a trendsetter were past. Within weeks he recorded "Body and Soul," which remains one of the definitive Jazz solos. What was equally remarkable was that this sophisticated improvisation struck a chord with the public and sold well. This commercial success led to his brief career as leader of a big band. It was during this period of the early to mid-forties that Hawkins actively encouraged Max Roach, Thelonious Monk, and Dizzy Gillespie, giving them jobs and recording dates when few saw their potential. By the late '40s, Hawkins was a key member of producer Norman Granz's organization and spent the rest of his life touring the world and recording. In the 1950s, Hawkins also began doing quintet jobs with trumpeter Roy Eldridge, some of which were recorded and are highlights of their discographies. Of the hundreds of sessions he made, other highlights include the 1943 "The Man I Love" and the 1947 "I Love You"; dates with Thelonious Monk (1957), Duke Ellington (1962), and Sonny Rollins (1963); and his own *Today and Now* (1962).

Joe Henderson (1937–2001): One of the most quirky and individual voices to appear on the tenor saxophone in the wake of Rollins and Coltrane, Henderson was rare in that his brilliant solos were not the be all and end all of his expression. His music always had an overall unity, and it was for this reason that his early albums quickly became classics (*Page One, Mode for Joe, Inner Urge,* and *Power to the People*) as did his compositions. Henderson established himself in the early and mid-sixties with the bands of Kenny Dorham and Horace Silver. In the decades following his year with Herbie Hancock (1969–70), Henderson remained true to his muse in his modest, unassuming yet impassioned way. Although he had some fallow years, Henderson exerted a significant influence on younger players during the '70s and '80s. His dedication paid off in the early 1990s, when he experienced a renaissance of sorts. This included some very high profile and musically rewarding albums saluting Billy Strayhorn (*Lush Life*), Miles Davis (*So Near, So Far*) and George Gershwin (*Porgy and Bess*).

Earl Hines (1903–83): The sheer audacity of pianist Hines's style renders terms such as "modern" meaningless. Jazz piano before Earl Hines was orchestral in nature and owed much to the conventions of European concert music. Hines took the filigree and decoration out and replaced it with an intensity and attack that could be savage at times. By 1928, Hines's approach to Jazz piano was as radical as Picasso's cubism was to traditional forms of representation. Leaving his native Pittsburgh for Chicago in 1923, Hines eventually struck up a seminal association with Louis Armstrong that resulted in a series of classic recordings that included "West End Blues," "Basin Street Blues," and "Muggles." As good as the band sides were, it was their duet on "Weatherbird" that captured their collaboration at its zenith. Ideas flew back and forth with dizzying speed as they inspired each other to new heights of invention. Hines also spent a good deal of time working with the legendary New Orleans clarinetist Jimmie Noone, and their recordings were also definitive ("Four or Five Times" and "Apex Blues"). In 1929, Hines became the leader of a big band, which—although based at Chicago's Grand Terrace Ballroom for a decade—toured, broadcast, recorded, and established a national reputation. The band had a hit in 1940 with "Boogie Woogie on St. Louis Blues," but many of their lesser-known recordings are truly superior ("Yellow Fire," "Cavernism," and "Tantalizing a Cuban"). One of his greatest bands, which included Charlie Parker, Dizzy Gillespie, Sarah Vaughan, and Billy Eckstine, was never recorded due to a musicians' recording strike. Hines joined Armstrong's All Stars in 1947, staying for four years before forming a series of small bands—a format he stayed with for the remainder of his life. He recorded in a variety of settings in the '70s, including a duet with violinist Joe Venuti and an inspired set of solo recordings.

Billie Holiday (1915–59): Defining a Jazz vocalist is almost as hard as defining what Jazz is, but no one would dispute that Billie Holiday (born Eleanora Fagan) is the definitive Jazz singer. Her approach was that of a Jazz instrumentalist. Tellingly, she was known early in her career for asking her accompanists to stop playing and repeat a given improvised passage if it contained something she thought she could use. It wasn't that the words were not important to her, but the gist of her art came from the sound of her voice and her rhythmic phrasing. This is not to imply that Holiday was not an actress when she sang, but the effect she gave was more a statement on the act of singing and an attitude than it was a reflection of the actual sentiment of the words. After a nightmare of a childhood and adolescence, Holiday attracted attention while performing in Harlem nightspots in the early '30s. From her earliest work with Benny Goodman in 1933 ("Your Mother's Son-in-Law"), Duke Ellington in 1934 ("Symphony in Black: Blues"), and Teddy Wilson in 1935 ("What a Little Moonlight Can Do"), she was clearly an individual and idiosyncratic stylist. Holiday forced the listener to hear her on her own terms—there is not even the slightest nod toward a "pretty" sound—and those terms were far from the norm at the time. By Holiday's own admission, she had listened carefully to Bessie Smith and Louis Armstrong, and forged her own inimitable style out of the amalgam. She worked with the bands of Count Basie in 1937 and Artie Shaw the following year, but she cemented her reputation with the many classic recordings she made during this period—the most influential of which featured tenor saxophonist Lester Young ("Me, Myself and I," "A Sailboat in the Moonlight," and "Without Your Love"). They found a way to spontaneously create counterpoint that has been equalled by few and surpassed by none. Holiday began appearing on her own in late 1938, and through the next two decades sustained many ups and (mostly) downs as her career was buffeted by the excesses of her addictions to alcohol and narcotics. But with the exception of a handful of sessions where she was clearly off form, the great bulk of her recorded legacy remains sublime. Highlights from the '40s include "There Is No Greater Love," "Deep Song," and "You're My Thrill." Producer Norman Granz surrounded her with her peers (including saxophonists Benny Carter and Ben Webster, and her favorite pianist Jimmy Rowles) for several first-class sessions in the mid-fifties that produced remakes of many of her classic recordings; they do not suffer in the least by comparison. Holiday had a striking reunion with Young as part of the classic 1957 television show *The Sound of Jazz*, and within two years' time they were both gone.

Freddie Hubbard (b. 1938): The possessor of a brilliant trumpet technique, a ravishing tone, and an adventurous way of improvising. Along with Miles Davis, Booker Little, and Woody Shaw, Hubbard shaped the way Jazz trumpet continues to be played to this day. There was something brash about Hubbard's playing when he arrived on the Jazz scene in 1959, and before long he was playing with J. J. Johnson, Slide Hampton, Sonny Rollins, and Quincy Jones. Not content to play in the accepted modes of the day, there seemed to be nothing he wouldn't try and Hubbard fit in naturally during classic recording sessions with Eric Dolphy, John Coltrane, and Ornette Coleman. He gained invaluable experience as a member of Art Blakey's band (1961–64), after which Hubbard became a bandleader, with the exception of a brief stint with Max Roach. His own series of recordings ("Ready for Freddie," "Hub-tones," and "Breaking Point") were notable for their stylistic unity and for the way in which they display Hubbard's growth as an improviser and as a composer. During the 1970s, Hubbard made several recordings in the rock, funk, and disco styles designed to reach a larger audience, none of which succeeded to any significant degree. Far more successful were the albums Red Clay, Straight Life, and V.S.O.P., where he was surrounded by his peers, many whom were ex–Miles Davis sidemen. His core following always remained the Jazz public, and by the '80s he returned largely to that format. Health problems have kept him mostly off the scene in the last decade.

Keith Jarrett (b. 1945): One of the freshest Jazz pianists and composers to come out of the 1960s. Jarrett has prodigious technical skills and an affinity for lyrical melodies that give his work a singing, at times yearning, quality. In addition, he is a visceral pianist who frequently mirrors his emotions with his entire body. After a brief spell with Art Blakey in 1966, Jarrett joined tenor saxophonist Charles Lloyd's quartet, where he gained international prominence. In 1969, Jarrett began a two-year association with Miles Davis, just as the trumpeter was easing into his electronic period. Jarrett is heard on electronic keyboards on both *Live at the Fillmore* and *Live/Evil*. During the '70s, Jarrett led two quartets. In the States, he appeared with Charlie Haden, Paul Motian, and Dewey Redman ("Treasure Island"). In Europe, he featured the saxophonist Jan Garbarek ("Belonging"). Both groups enjoyed great popularity, addressed a wide range of styles, and were resolutely acoustic at a time when electric instruments were in vogue. Jarrett also began appearing as a piano soloist, improvising entire concerts that occasionally approached prolixity but nonetheless achieved a feeling of form and structure. The recordings of these mammoth efforts (*The Sun Bear Concerts*) were also very successful. Classical music has become a passion of Jarrett's, as has a trio with bassist Gary Peacock and drummer Jack DeJohnette that plays a classic repertoire of Jazz standards.

J. J. Johnson (1924–2001): Few musicians had a greater effect on their instrument than J. J. (given name, James Lewis) Johnson did on the trombone. Though there were many virtuosic and fleet trombonists before him, Johnson took as much of the slide out of the sound of the trombone as possible. A gifted composer and arranger, Johnson played with Benny Carter's band (1942–45) and learned much about the intricacies of the music from Carter, who was beginning to establish himself as one of the first black film composers in Hollywood. Johnson moved to Los Angeles twenty-five years later and became a busy composer for films and television. He played with Count Basie and Illinois Jacquet after leaving Carter's band, and recorded with Charlie Parker's quintet in 1947 (*Crazeology*). Many listeners thought he was playing a valve trombone because of the fluidity and trumpetlike phrasing he achieved. Troubled by the difficulty in raising a family and being a traveling Jazz musician, Johnson took a position as a blueprint inspector from 1952–54, though he continued to record classic sessions with Miles Davis. His solos on "Blue 'N Boogie" and "Walkin' " are among his greatest. Johnson returned to music full-time with a quintet co-led with fellow trombonist Kai Winding, called Jay and Kai. It was tremendously successful, and established Johnson as a major Jazz attraction. Their music tread a fine line between Jazz and commercial music, and when they broke up in 1956, Johnson quickly formed a new band that included pianist Tommy Flanagan and drummer Elvin Jones. He remained a leader from then on, distinguishing his groups with well-organized, concise arrangements (*The Complete J. J. Johnson Small*

Groups on Columbia). Johnson grew as a composer, writing pieces for large ensembles ("Poem for Brass" and "El Camino Real") including the 1961 "Perceptions" for Dizzy Gillespie. After spending almost twenty years in Hollywood, Johnson returned to his native Indianapolis, where he concentrated on composing, relieved by occasional touring and recording. In later years, his playing became noticeably warmer, which can be heard on the albums *Tangence* and *Heroes*.

James P. Johnson (1894–1955): A seminal influence who, more than anyone else, created stride piano. Using a virtuosic foundation based on the European model, the young James P. integrated elements from the church, ragtime, and blues into his piano style. He was an exceptional composer ("The Charleston" and "If I Could Be with You" were two of his biggest hits) and could create a seemingly limitless number of spontaneous variations on a theme. Johnson's style played a large role in the development of Duke Ellington, Fats Waller, Count Basie, and Thelonious Monk. His piano solos ("Mule Walk" and "Carolina Shout," for instance) were required of any upcoming pianist in the 1920s. Johnson was also a superlative and creative band pianist, as can be heard on a series of recordings made between 1938 and 1945 ("Swingin' at the Lido" and "After You've Gone"). Johnson spent the latter part of his career trying to be recognized as a composer of extended pieces, which included suites, symphonies, and operas. While these works do not bear favorable comparison to his shorter masterpieces, they bespeak a man not satisfied to rest on his laurels.

Elvin Jones (b. 1927): One of the most influential and immediately identifiable drummers in Jazz, Jones introduced a new approach that drew heavily on the polyrhythms that distinguish African music. Basically, what Jones managed to do was to add another layer of rhythm on top of the basic Jazz beat and move freely back and forth between these two pulses. Since the swing feeling that defines Jazz comes from the juxtaposition of duple (2/4 or 4/4) and triple meters (3/4), this gave Jones an unprecedented number of expressive options. There had been moves in this direction before, most notably from the master drummers Shadow Wilson and Roy Haynes. The younger brother of pianist Hank and cornetist/composer Thad, Elvin's playing was the source of much confusion when he arrived in New York in the mid-fifties. He established himself as member of trombonist J. J. Johnson's quintet, but many players took his budding originality for incompetence. More high-level work with Sonny Rollins ("A Night at the Vanguard"), Stan Getz, and Harry "Sweets" Edison prepared Jones for what was to be the pairing of a lifetime. There have been a handful of horn players and drummers who together created a unique rhythmic synergy. John Coltrane and Elvin Jones enabled each other to reach previously unexplored areas of Jazz expression that remain among the most impassioned and influential works in the music's history. Many of Coltrane's Quartet's performances developed into a saxophone and drum duet that went on for extended periods. Any of the quartet's many recordings feature these moments—one of the most classic ones is *Live at Birdland*. Jones became a bandleader after leaving Coltrane in 1965, and he continues to lead distinguished groups. One of the most amazing things about Jones's playing, known for its ferocity, is that he has always been a master of the brushes; and even when using the sticks, he plays with great restraint and at a relatively modest dynamic level most of the time. A series of trio recordings with pianist Tommy Flanagan showcases the more traditional side of Jones's art and makes for a fascinating comparison with his own recordings as a leader.

Lee Konitz (b. 1927): There have been precious few truly original voices in the history of Jazz, and alto saxophonist Lee Konitz certainly belongs in that select group. It only takes a few notes of his gentle, lyrical sound to identify him. However, there is nothing "soft" about his music, and its designation as "cool" has ultimately served as an obstacle. Originally a member of the cultlike group of young musicians who gathered around pianist Lennie Tristano, Konitz broke out on his own and quickly expanded his musical horizons. Konitz came to prominence at a time when virtually every young alto player sounded like a version of Charlie Parker. It was Konitz's great gift to arrive at his own style early on, and he has continued to hone it for more than half a century. Konitz phrases evenly most of the time, and his reverence for Bach comes across in the purity of his improvised lines. His recorded solos with Tristano ("Crosscurrents"), Miles Davis ("Godchild"), and Stan Kenton, and those recorded under his own name, became études for many aspiring players. Konitz led his own bands from then on, making many recordings, and pairing up every now and then with his ex-Tristano band mate tenor saxophonist Warne Marsh, with whom he shared an aesthetic bond that led them to sound at times like one person. Konitz has always thrived on new and challenging musical situations. Commercially, this has worked against him, giving the public too little to hold on to in terms of an established musical profile, but that very quality is at the root of his greatness. Konitz feels that most Jazz musicians do not truly improvise, so to make sure that he does, he creates these ever-changing bands that remove any chance for playing by rote on his part. This has resulted in one of the largest and most diverse recorded legacies of any Jazz musician, *Motion* and *Duets*, which forms the bulk of his legacy.

John Lewis (1920–2001): The creator of the Modern Jazz Quartet, a superlative composer, and an original and provocative pianist, Lewis grew up in Albuquerque, encountered Lester Young and Duke Ellington there, and studied anthropology at the University of New Mexico. After serving in World War II, Lewis came to New York, where he quickly began performing and arranging for Dizzy Gillespie's big band. There was a circle of musicians who wanted to broaden what they felt was bop's rather limited scope. They gathered around the arranger Gil Evans, and it was from this group that the Miles Davis Nonet emerged. Lewis both played and arranged for the band ("Rouge" and "Move"). While completing his master's degree at Manhattan School of Music, Lewis worked around New York and made classic recordings with Charlie Parker and Lester Young. Both in his compositions and at the keyboard, Lewis reveled in counterpoint, and became one of the few true masters of this challenging method Jazz has produced. All of Lewis's abilities found their ultimate expression in the MJQ. Working with three great players (vibraphonist

Milt Jackson, bassist Percy Heath, and drummer Kenny Clarke, later replaced by Connie Kay), Lewis organized their material down to the finest detail, without ever losing his passion for blues and swing. A representative sampling of their best recordings would include the albums *The Comedy*, *European Concert*, and *Blues on Bach*. They stayed together until 1976 and soon began a series of regular reunions that lasted until the deaths of Kay and Jackson in the 1990s. Lewis also composed film scores, orchestral music, and ballet scores, and retained his artistic integrity for over half a century.

Booker Little (1938–61): Jazz has had more than its share of great musicians who died far too soon, but it is hard to think of a more tragic case than that of trumpeter Booker Little. In a span of just over three years, Little created a significant legacy whose influence continues. Little came to prominence as a member of Max Roach's band. He had been brought to Roach's attention by none other than Sonny Rollins. Little's playing had a brilliance and technical panache that bore a surface similarity to that of the then recently departed Clifford Brown. But Little was his own man, with a particular talent for ferreting out musical dissonances that other players had ignored, and using them to great effect. Little plays an important role in several albums with Roach's band, including the classic *Percussion Bittersweet*. Like the very greatest players, just his sound alone in an ensemble could be very moving. Little made four albums under his own name. The last, aptly titled *Victory and Sorrow*, recorded just a couple of months before his death, contains some of his greatest playing.

Joe Lovano (b. 1952): One of the major saxophonists and band-leaders of today as well as a skilled percussionist. Lovano is at home in virtually every genre of Jazz, and has found a personal language in the Jazz idiom that transcends any and all stylistic dialects. After years in the big bands of Woody Herman and Mel Lewis, Lovano began to attract attention as a deep thinker with the issuance of his first small-group album *Tones, Shapes and Colors*. Not interested in mere blowing sessions, Lovano strives for and maintains a compositional unity that raises the level of his music markedly. A fine drummer himself, Lovano has always surrounded himself with the best rhythm sections. Pianist Kenny Werner and drummer Ed Blackwell are just two of the giants who have worked and recorded with Lovano. He was also a member of a trio with Paul Motian and guitarist Bill Frisell that was one of the few truly innovative bands of the 1980s. For over a decade, he has been producing a series of challenging and varied "concept" albums. Highlights include the orchestral *Rush Hour* with Gunther Schuller, *Celebrating Sinatra* and *52nd Street Themes* (the two most straight-ahead), and *Trio Fascination—Edition One* with Dave Holland and Elvin Jones.

Wynton Marsalis (b. 1961): This New Orleans trumpeter, band-leader, and composer is unique in Jazz in the sense that he enjoys a solid reputation in classical music and is also acknowledged to be an original and tremendously influential Jazz musician. Marsalis's recordings of the classical trumpet literature established him as a major attraction while he was still in his teens. After moving to New York to attend the Juilliard School, he joined Art Blakey's band along with his brother, saxophonist Branford. During the course of the 1980s, Marsalis matured, and by mid-decade was recording Jazz albums that were both popular and innovative. *Black Codes from the Underground* and *Blue Interlude* are outstanding examples of this trumpeter's ability to shape a band through his own playing and writing into a unit that is highly polished, yet retains an edge of spontaneity. By this time, Marsalis was using the bully pulpit of his fame to inspire young Jazz musicians to seriously address the music's tradition as he sees it; and from this flowered a generation of players whose personal visions have ranged far and wide. As the artistic director of Jazz at Lincoln Center, Marsalis has, naturally enough, come into his share of controversy. He has remained a prolific composer ("In This House," "On This Morning," "Citi Movement," and "The Marciac Suite") with a pronounced capacity to write counterpoint, and won the first Pulitzer Prize to go to a Jazz musician for his epic *Blood on the Fields*.

Charles Mingus (1922–79): Like Ellington and Jelly Roll Morton, bassist Mingus was one of the great personalities of his time, and a distinguished composer/bandleader. The problem in assessing innovators is that the more influential they are, the harder it is to appreciate just how daring their concepts originally were. Many of the ideas Mingus introduced in the '50s have become commonplace in the Jazz of today. As a bassist, Charles Mingus raised the ante enormously by shunning the standard modes of accompaniment. This is evident even in his 1950–51 recordings with the Red Norvo Trio. But he was fated not to be a sideman, and although Mingus had already led his own groups on the West Coast in the 1940s, it wasn't until he moved to New York in the early '50s that he gained the kind of exposure he deserved. As a composer and band-leader, Mingus placed an emphasis on counterpoint and on radical tempo and mood changes. He also explicitly addressed social issues such as racism at a time when that was just not done. Mingus was one of the most significant Jazz composers to emerge after Ellington. For twenty years, he produced a series of outstanding albums that featured many of the best improvisers of the time (among the first were Jackie McLean, Jimmy Knepper, Eric Dolphy, Booker Ervin, John Handy, and Roland Hanna) and he consistently questioned what most Jazz players considered common practice. Mingus was given to writing programmatic music, and some of his most classic recordings include "Tijuana Moods," "Better Git It in Your Soul," "The Clown," and "The Black Saint and the Sinner Lady." He was also a tremendously volatile person who phys-ically attacked some of his musicians and, on occasion, his audience. There have been many articles and even a film made about him that explore these facets of his personality. What remains now is the music and the example of someone who gave his life to his art.

Thelonious Monk (1917–82): Everything about pianist/composer Thelonious Sphere Monk was startlingly original. His melo-dies were spiky and dissonant yet memorable and, for the most part, singable. As a pianist, Monk broke all the rules of touch, fingering, and posture, yet he was in many ways one of Art Tatum's most profound disciples. At the root of his musical genius was an ability to create variations based on the melody of the piece he was playing. That may not sound like an earth-shattering achievement, but during a time when Jazz was evolving more and more into a harmonically based music, Monk's concentration on its melodic aspect was a revelation. Like those of Tatum, Monk's solos always remained hinged to the melody, and they also shared a rare ability to abstract a tune while enhancing its essence, rather than parodying it. In the early 1940s, Monk was in the house band at Minton's Playhouse, which also included drummer Kenny Clarke. Among the musicians who sat in regularly were Charlie Christian and Dizzy Gillespie, and Monk was integrally involved in the new music that evolved there. Coleman Hawkins was one of a very few established musicians who encouraged Monk, hiring him to play on 52nd Street and to record. For the next decade, Monk rarely worked but recorded occasionally and was best known for his composition "Round Midnight," which became a Jazz standard. Monk's career finally took off in the mid-fifties with a series of classic albums for the Riverside label (*Monk Plays Ellington, Brilliant Corners, Monk at Town Hall*). His quartet's engagement at New York's Five Spot Café (with John Coltrane on tenor saxophone) in 1957 was tremendously successful and led directly to a major recording label contract, constant touring, and, eventually, the cover of *Time* magazine. Plagued by ever-increasing spells of a manic-depressive disorder, Monk gradually withdrew from performing in the mid-seventies.

Jelly Roll Morton (1890–1941): A character right out of Twain or Dickens: a legendary liar who could nonetheless back up many of his claims; the first great Jazz composer and a first-rate pianist who claimed to have single-handedly invented

Jazz in 1902 (Morton was rare in that he claimed to be five years older than he actually was); a sometime pimp; and the source of one of the great oral histories of American music. Morton (born Ferdinand Lamothe) had a great beat and was a prime figure in merging the blues tradition with ragtime. Though many of his compositions have structures that reflect the multithemed legacy of ragtime, Morton's integration of improvisation and the blues took them into a new and distinctly different musical sphere. Of all his many accomplishments, Morton's greatest contribution to Jazz was his ability to capture on paper the free-flowing polyphony of New Orleans music. Recordings such as "Grandpa's Spells," "Black Bottom Stomp," and "The Pearls" are as close to perfection as any Jazz performances to this day. His band was called the Red Hot Peppers, and Morton enjoyed his greatest popularity when these records came out in 1926. A few of Morton's tunes became standards during the Big Band Era ("King Porter Stomp," "Wolverine Blues," and "Milenberg Joys") and the fact that he had sold most of the rights to them years earlier fueled his frustration, which certainly contributed to his early death. Morton recorded several hours of his memories—when telling stories, as has been noted by many writers, he sounds like the kind of liar who doesn't expect to be believed—for musicologist Alan Lomax in 1938, and excerpts of these recordings were eventually issued. They are one of the most important documents ever recorded about the evolution of Jazz and have been in print in various incarnations for decades. Morton had traveled the country early in the century and had a great ear and a great memory. The veracity of his tales is secondary to the flavor and essence they capture in revealing how Jazz was born.

Gerry Mulligan (1927–96): A baritone saxophonist and composer/bandleader who was one of the handful of Jazzmen to become a household name in the 1950s. His pianoless quartet featuring trumpeter Chet Baker created a sensation in the early '50s with its clean, spare sound and the way the horns and the bass and drums interacted with each other. Mulligan established his reputation, however, with his fresh writing for the bands of Elliot Lawrence, Gene Krupa, and Claude Thornhill. He emphasized long-lined melodies that straddled the horn sections in new ways. But it was the end of the Big Band Era, and Mulligan turned his attention to smaller bands. He was a major voice both as player and arranger/composer for the Miles Davis Nonet (1949–50), which, for all its subsequent influence and renown, played only a handful of gigs and completed just three recording dates. Mulligan's "Jeru" and "Rocker" made the nine-piece band sound full and complete through innovative combinations of instruments and a penchant for a relaxed and flowing rhythmic approach that owed much to Lester Young and the Thornhill band. It was the quartet with Baker that caught the public's ear, and Mulligan led small bands throughout the 1950s. Two of the best were a sextet with Bob Brookmeyer, Jon Eardley, and Zoot Sims, and a quartet with Art Farmer that made the classic *What Is There to Say?* album. Essential to all of these groups was Mulligan's ability to spontaneously weave counterpoint throughout entire performances. He mixed written segments with improvised ones in such a fashion that both the audiences and his fellow musicians were kept on their toes. In addition, Mulligan was able to get his sidemen to listen and interact with this unusual style—which was not the way the great majority of Jazz was played at the time. Despite his small group's tremendous success in the late '50s, Mulligan's heart remained with the big bands, and he formed the Concert Jazz Band in 1960. He surrounded himself with the best players and writers, including Bob Brookmeyer ("I Know, Don't Know How") and Gary McFarland ("Weep"), made some classic recordings, and made a few tours, but the project lost steam a few years later. From that point on, Mulligan devoted himself to varied projects, appearing with Dave Brubeck, writing film scores, and putting together various-sized bands for the occasional tour and/or recording session. Later in life, he wrote orchestral music, including a piece which he played with the New York Philharmonic.

Joe "King" Oliver (1885–1938): Throughout his life, Louis Armstrong insisted that all he was doing was playing music in the style of his mentor, New Orleans cornetist Oliver. While this may very well have been what Armstrong was hearing, it functions more as a testament to his regard for Oliver than as an influence we can discern. In a town known for its boisterous and frequently blaring trumpet kings, Oliver was revered for his finesse and taste. While he could certainly blast it out when he chose, Oliver favored a wide dynamic range both on his cornet and with his various bands that included playing so softly that he could hear the women's feet as they danced on the floor. After leading one of the top bands in the

Crescent City in the teens, Oliver flitted between Chicago and the West Coast before settling in Chicago and making his first recordings in 1923. His Creole Jazz Band featured the best of the transplanted New Orleans musicians, including Armstrong, who made his first recordings with the band ("Chimes Blues," "Dippermouth Blues," and "Tears"). Oliver was already experiencing the tooth and general health problems that led to his early decline, and consequently, never recorded in peak form. But the early duets with Jelly Roll Morton ("King Porter Stomp") give us as good a glimpse as we are going to get of what entranced Armstrong. Oliver's manipulation of mutes to produce different sounds is especially interesting (as is the fact that his greatest disciple, Armstrong, largely eschewed mutes). He led bands in New York and recorded a series in which he plays infrequently and inconsistently, though there are a handful of beautifully poignant moments ("What You Want Me to Do"). A long series of bad business decisions—he turned down the Cotton Club engagement that made Duke Ellington's career—left Oliver leading a road band of unknown players in the early '30s that included Lester Young, who, significantly, remembered Oliver's blues playing. Though Armstrong tried to help him when he could, Oliver died in obscurity, working as a janitor in a pool hall.

Walter Page (1900–57): Known primarily as the bassist in the original Count Basie band, Page was a prime mover in the evolution of Kansas City Jazz. He was known as "Big 'Un" to his peers, a testament not only to his physical stature, but also to his preeminence as a teacher and bandleader of great renown. In the late '20s, Page imparted his concept to his own band, the Blue Devils, and they achieved a reputation of mythic proportions before they were stolen away, one by one, by his rival, bandleader Bennie Moten, who had the patronage of the town's legendary mayor, Tom Pendergast, behind him. Page played the tuba and baritone saxophone with the same authority he displayed on the string bass, and when he finally threw in the towel and joined Moten in 1932, the stage was set for one of the truly defining moments in Jazz history. Page's propulsion of the band, along with Eddie Durham's discoveries in the realm of swinging Jazz orchestration, resulted in the one of the first innovations to be made away from New York, where the pace had been set by Duke Ellington, Benny Carter, and Bill Challis. There is no precedent in Jazz for their fiery recordings of "Lafayatte," "Prince of Wails," and "Toby." Page not only played superlative bass on these recordings, but also brought to bear his musical philosophy of making the rhythm flow. The Depression hit all of these territory bands very hard, and Page never led a band again. But he remained the *éminence grise* in the Basie band throughout his long tenure with them (1936–47, with a few years off during the war years). He can be heard to great advantage on any number of small-group sessions with Lester Young and Basie, and is featured on the 1938 Kansas City Six recording of "Pagin' the Devil." Page spent his remaining years freelancing, mostly with fellow ex-Basieites.

Charlie Parker (1920–55): Alto saxophonist Parker may very well be the most influential Jazz improviser after Louis Armstrong. His influence remains as strong today as it was when he died, almost a half century ago. Parker was born and raised in and around Kansas City and brought a deep feeling for blues and swing to everything he played, no matter how fast the tempo or how complex his harmonic variations became. Parker was the subject of a well-intentioned but seriously flawed 1988 Hollywood biopic that painted him as musically illiterate. Those who knew him paint a portrait of a brilliant man who struggled unsuccessfully with drug addiction from his late teens. Parker made his first commercial recordings with Jay McShann's band in 1941 ("Sepian Bounce" and "Jumpin' the Blues") and while they reveal an original voice within the general parameters of Lester Young's style, it wasn't until Parker appeared on a series of epochal small-group sessions with trumpeter Dizzy Gillespie in 1945 ("Hot House," "Salt Peanuts," and "Lover Man") that the true import of his genius became manifest. In the remaining decade of his life, Parker became increasingly notorious for his extra-musical exploits, but his talent never deserted him, and there are dozens of classic recordings from each of those years—some recorded surreptitiously on the gig, and others in the studio. Parker was a classicist whose improvisations were for the most part well ordered, played with immaculate precision, and largely within the boundaries of the established Jazz tradition. At the heart of his music was a rhythmic freedom combined with a penchant for melodic phrases. Those phrases inspired Miles Davis, John Coltrane, and many others who, in turn, bring us right into our contemporary Jazz world. "Parker's Mood," "Embraceable You," "Now's the Time," and dozens of other timeless Parker recordings contain solos that echo across the Jazz world daily. Among his large discography, the

1950 (*Bird 'N Diz*) and 1953 reunions (*Jazz at Massey Hall*) with Gillespie stand out, as do his sessions with a string section (*Just Friends*).

Jaco Pastorius (1951–87): An electric bassist/bandleader/composer who was precociously talented and burned out far too young from a combination of mental and drug-related problems, Pastorius had an unprecedented instrumental virtuosity on the electric bass and was a sophisticated composer, in addition to being a wildly charismatic performer. An early job with Pat Metheny led to an extended period with Weather Report; he became a prime voice in the band, alongside its founders Wayne Shorter and Joe Zawinul. It soon became clear that he was redefining the role of his instrument in the same way that Jimmy Blanton had with Ellington, and Pastorius was soon in demand as a studio sideman. He made his first album as a leader in 1976 (*Jaco Pastorius*), and included a solo version of "Donna Lee" and a wide array of music that reflected his eclectic tastes. In 1981, Pastorius formed Word of Mouth and became a full-time bandleader. They played everything from Bach to the Beatles, and surprisingly it came off without sounding forced. The group varied in size and instrumentation, at times coming close to a traditional big band (Invitation). By the mid-eighties, everything had fallen apart for Pastorius, and his death robbed Jazz of a musician who had achieved a rare blend of art and commercialism.

Oscar Pettiford (1922–60): A bassist who had continued the innovations set in motion by Jimmy Blanton, though it is more than likely that Pettiford would have been tilling the same field whether there had been a Blanton or not. A member of a large musical family based in Oklahoma, Pettiford was inspired by guitarist Charlie Christian, whose flowing style he adapted to the bass in the late '30s. After coming to New York with Charlie Barnet's band in 1943, Pettiford became an early associate of Dizzy Gillespie and they co-led a fabled band on 52nd Street where their new music first gained wide exposure. Personality conflicts put Pettiford out on his own, and he became the bassist of choice, winding up in Coleman Hawkins's band, where he recorded his first solo ("The Man I Love"), which immediately became a classic. A two-year stint with Ellington followed, and then the beginnings of his career as a bandleader (Pettiford was also a fine composer). In early 1949, Pettiford led a band that included (at various times) Fats Navarro, Miles Davis, Bud Powell, and Milt Jackson, but bass players (with the exception of John Kirby, who never featured himself) were not considered frontmen. There followed a short stay with Woody Herman's band, where he broke his arm, and it was while recuperating that Pettiford began playing the cello. Ellington gave Pettiford a recording session of his own to feature the new instrument and the Charlie Christian influence was even more apparent than it had been on the bass ("Perdido" and "Take the 'A' Train"). As his reputation grew, Pettiford began to lead groups again, culminating in a big band that appeared around New York and which made a few first-rate albums (*Deep Passion*). He also appeared on recording dates with Thelonious Monk, Miles Davis, and Lucky Thompson, and was to many the most eloquent bass soloist of the era. Frustrated at the lack of work for his own bands, Pettiford expatriated to Europe in 1958 and worked frequently with Stan Getz, Bud Powell, and Kenny Clarke.

Bud Powell (1924–66): The major influence in Jazz piano during the mid-forties, Powell created a new idiom that used the left hand as accompanist to the right hand, which spun out long, Charlie Parker–like lines. The most important thing about Powell was not the particulars of his piano style, but the sheer confidence and brilliance of his improvisations. He first recorded with Cootie Williams's big band in 1944, and Thelonious Monk became his mentor. Drummer Kenny Clarke claimed that many of Monk's pieces from that period were written with Powell in mind. There has always been an element of "what if" about Powell's career. He had severe mental problems that were exacerbated by head injuries received in a racial incident in 1945. There were to be long periods of hospitalization and erratic performances for the rest of his life; but when Powell was "on," he was like a force of nature. Two trio recordings in particular, one from 1947 ("Somebody Loves Me") and one from 1951 ("Un Poco Loco") feature Powell (and drummer Max Roach) in superlative form. There was also a 1953 concert date (*Jazz at Massey Hall*) with Charlie Parker, Dizzy Gillespie, Charles Mingus, and Roach that has several flowing Powell solos. But it was not just his solos that were exceptional. His manner of accompaniment, with jabbing chords played largely in the piano's middle register, created a perpetual harmonic rhythm that was imitated for decades. It should be noted that Dizzy Gillespie claimed to have taught this to Powell. There were more recordings and international touring before Powell settled in Paris in 1959.

His condition deteriorated, and although there were rare returns to his old form, most notably a reunion with Coleman Hawkins, Oscar Pettiford, and Clarke (*Essen Jazz Festival Concert*), Powell gave up performing in the last period of his life.

Dewey Redman (b. 1931): The advent of Ornette Coleman opened the door for a generation of homemade Jazz musicians who could not deal with the music's sophisticated heritage; saxophonist Dewey Redman was clearly not one of those. A master of blues and of melodic swing, Redman brought a fresh approach to boyhood friend Coleman's freewheeling musical world ("New York Is Now" and "Love Call") in the late '60s and early '70s. Although he is not nearly as celebrated as many of his peers (or his son Joshua, for that matter), Redman is a unique figure whose influence can be heard through many younger players, including Joe Lovano. During the '70s, Redman was featured with Charlie Haden's Liberation Orchestra, but his great exposure came during his years with Keith Jarrett (*The Survivor's Suite*). Charlie Haden and Paul Motian were also in this band, and they made some of the freshest music of that decade. He spent the next decade appearing with Old and New Dreams, which reunited Coleman's groundbreaking quartet (Don Cherry, Haden, and Ed Blackwell) with Redman in the leader's place. Two late '90s recordings show the extraordinary range of this underappreciated master—*In London*, where he plays a handful of standards (and does an uncanny tribute to Dexter Gordon on one tune) and the uneven but nonetheless fascinating trio session with Cecil Taylor and Elvin Jones (*Momentum Space*).

Django Reinhardt (1910–53): A radically fresh Jazz guitarist who proved beyond a doubt that Jazz was indeed a fine art with no boundaries. A gypsy who came to fame in France in the '30s, Reinhardt had been transfixed by Louis Armstrong's 1930 recording of the "Dallas Blues." Within a few years, he evolved an innovative style that was all the more astonishing for the fact that his right hand had been badly disfigured in a fire, and he accomplished all of his virtuosic figures with only a few fingers. In the sheer idiosyncrasy and originality of his style, Reinhardt presages Thelonious Monk; but unlike Monk, Reinhardt was a relatively overnight sensation. His group, the Quintet of the Hot Club of France, was a featured attraction in Europe throughout the '30s, and its records also sold well in the United States. The band's other featured soloist was violinist Stephane Grappelli, whose suave urbanity made a wonderful contrast with the guitarist's unorthodox stylings. Reinhardt recorded prolifically with the Quintet ("Nuages" and "Sweet Sue"), with the expatriate Americans Benny Carter and Coleman Hawkins ("Sweet Georgia Brown" and "Crazy Rhythm"), Dicky Wells ("Between the Devil and the Deep Blue Sea"), and with a small group from the touring Ellington band, which included Rex Stewart ("Monmartre" and "Finesse"). The war broke up the Quintet, and Reinhardt played in various groups, even recording with a big band. By this time, he was playing the electric guitar, and the concert recordings with Ellington ("Ride, Red, Ride") and the sessions he made with groups back in France show that he was thoroughly conversant with the new idioms of Gillespie and Parker. There were occasional reunions with Grappelli before his death. He remains an influence and offers guitarists fresh options outside of the Charlie Christian–derived style (it should be noted that Christian himself was said to have played Reinhardt solos from memory) from which the great majority of the instrument's heritage has evolved.

Max Roach (b. 1924): A gifted percussionist, composer, and bandleader who made quantum leaps in Jazz drumming in the '40s and '50s. One of the less fortunate offshoots that came from the intersection of Jazz and the entertainment world was the image of the drummer as a rhythm-crazed maniac who was anything but an intellectual. Max Roach obliterated that cliché with his serious yet unfailingly swinging discoveries. First as a sideman with Charlie Parker and then as a leader, Roach developed a manner of both accompaniment and soloing that created a new vocabulary for his instrument ("Klactoveesedstene" and "Klaunstance"). He could also play freely and with humor at the most outrageously fast tempos that Parker would call. Roach became the drummer of choice for virtually every major player of the era, recording prolifically as a sideman throughout the late '40s and early '50s. Equally at home in a trio with Bud Powell ("Un Poco Loco") and in Miles Davis's Nonet ("Move"), Roach played like a master orchestrator, using his brilliant and innovative technique to serve the music. In 1954, he formed a quintet along with the brilliant (and short-lived) young trumpeter Clifford Brown. They both flowered in this setting, and every one of the dozens of titles they recorded contains a collection of definitive moments in Jazz percussion ("Joy Spring," "I Get a Kick Out of You," and "Mildama"). Over the course of the next decade, Roach pioneered the use of different meters and of using a tuba in a modern Jazz small group. He also introduced many young players who were to become major figures, including the trumpeter Booker Little. His music took on an overtly political stance against the insanity of racism as well, and from this came the classic *Freedom Now Suite*, which also featured his soon-to-be-wife, vocalist Abbey Lincoln. Never one to be defined by a preexisting model, Roach branched out in subsequent decades, collaborating with artists in many different genres, including dance. He composed for string quartets and films, lectured and taught internationally, created his percussion ensemble M'Boom, played duets with a wide range of partners, which have included Dizzy Gillespie and Cecil Taylor, and perfected a series of unaccompanied drum solos dedicated to his mentors, including Big Sid Catlett and Jo Jones.

Sonny Rollins (b. 1930): Besides being a primary influence on Jazz tenor saxophonists for half a century, Rollins is also one of the most brilliant improvisers in the music's history, regardless of instrument. Rollins grew up in Harlem and got to know his idol, Coleman Hawkins, while still a teenager. Many of Rollins's peers had to sacrifice much of the tenor saxophone's robust tonal quality in order to deal with the new challenges in velocity heralded in Charlie Parker's music. Rollins found a way to integrate what he loved so much in the playing of Hawkins, Lester Young, and Don Byas with his own burgeoning innovations. During the '50s, he recorded a series of classic albums with Miles Davis, Max Roach, and Thelonious Monk, and several under his own name—with the 1956 *Saxophone Colossus* and 1958 *Freedom Suite* remaining unsurpassed as sheer demonstrations of improvisational genius. The advent of John Coltrane and Ornette Coleman presented a tremendous challenge to Rollins's stature and to his own sense of being au courant. This led him to take what would be the first in a series of lengthy sabbaticals from public performance. The 1960s saw another spate of classic recordings with groups that ran the gamut from classicism (*The Bridge*) to experimentation (*East Broadway Rundown*) to music used for a film score (*Alfie*). Since the early 1970s, there has been a divergence between the Rollins of the recording studio, when he sounds inhibited, and the live Rollins, when he remains at any given moment one of the greatest Jazz players on the planet.

George Russell (b. 1923): The composer and pianist who created some of the most original Jazz compositions of the 1950s using the "Lydian Chromatic Concept of Tonal Organization," a system he devised to assist Jazz musicians in finding new avenues for tonal creativity. Originally a drummer, Russell devoted himself to composition in the late '40s, and his works were recorded by Dizzy Gillespie ("Cubano Be" and "Cubano Bop"), Artie Shaw, and Buddy DeFranco. It was in the mid-fifties that he blossomed into a major Jazz voice with his extended compositions "All About Rosie" (featuring pianist Bill Evans in his breakthrough performance) and the *New York, New York* suite. Though his pieces were direct offshoots of his Lydian theories, there is nothing in the slightest bit doctrinaire about them. Indeed, it is a mystery why Russell's work has not become a standard part of the Jazz canon, or why his works have not been rediscovered by the Jazz rep-

ertory movement. In the early '60s, he made a series of recordings with his sextet that included at times Don Ellis and
Eric Dolphy, of which "Ezz-Thctics" is a highlight. Russell
gradually drifted toward electronic instruments and a discur-
sive compositional style. His "Electronic Sonata for Souls
Loved by Nature 1980" is representative of where Russell has
gone. A longtime faculty member at the New England Con-
servatory, Russell continues to lead his Living Time Orchestra.

Eddie Sauter (1914–81): One of the most original voices in Jazz
composition to emerge in the wake of Duke Ellington. His
1936–38 writing for xylophonist Red Norvo's band (much of
it featuring Norvo's wife, vocalist Mildred Bailey) was startlingly fresh and subtle. Sauter's recasting of tunes such as
"Remember" and "Now It Can Be Told" are virtual recom-
positions, and sound like no one else. A fan of Shostakovitch,
Ellington, and Beethoven (among others), Sauter eschewed
the harmonic and orchestrational conventions of Jazz and developed his own language, which relied heavily on counterpoint, modulations, and new instrumental combinations. This
led him to Benny Goodman's band in 1939, where he gave
the band its first new direction since its inception in the
Benny Carter/Fletcher Henderson mold four years earlier
("Benny Rides Again," "More Than You Know," "Super-
man," and "How Deep Is the Ocean"). Sauter contracted tuberculosis from Charlie Christian during this period, and the
ensuing health problems curtailed his career during the war
years. He had a hard time reconciling his aesthetic sense with
his place in the commercial music world, and did anonymous

studio work while at the same time creating a series of masterpieces for the mid-forties bands of Artie Shaw ("Summertime" and "The Maid with the Flaccid Air") and Ray McKinley ("McKinley for President," "Idiot's Delight," and "Hangover Square"). In the '50s, he co-led a marvelous orchestra with another great arranger/composer with a decidedly uncommercial bent, Bill Finegan, that made several albums for RCA Victor that have largely fallen out of print for decades. Most contemporary Jazz fans know Sauter for the justly celebrated masterpiece *Focus*, an album he wrote for Stan Getz and a string ensemble. This led to a film score with the same crew (*Mickey One*). He continued to make his living, however, doing what he considered drudgework. A late masterpiece is his "Saxophone Quartet," which has recently been recorded by Ensemble Accanto & Xasax.

Maria Schneider (b. 1960): Though she has only made a few recordings under her own name ("Evanescence," "Coming About," and "Allegresse"), Schneider is a leading light as a big bandleader/composer/arranger. Gifted with a light touch in her orchestrations and a penchant for impressionist sounds, she has taken the legacy of her mentors (Bob Brookmeyer and Gil Evans) and created her own style. Her music tends to be through-composed and goes great distances to get away from the melody-solos-melody format that has overtaken so much of Jazz since the demise of the Big Band Era. For several years, Schneider's band had a weekly gig in New York City, where they had a chance to attain the kind of unity of purpose and consistency that specially assembled or infrequently working bands never achieve. And although her band consisted of musicians who also played in other groups, she managed to coax a unique ensemble sound out of them— another mark of a great leader. Her most outstanding soloists include trumpeter Greg Gisbert and saxophonists Rick Margitza and Scott Robinson.

Archie Shepp (b. 1937): A tenor saxophonist and bandleader who was a major figure in the "avant-garde" movement of the '60s, Shepp came to Jazz in a radically different way than most. He already had a degree in dramatic literature before he came to New York in the late 1950s and had had plays published and produced. Shepp quickly established himself on the tenor saxophone with the avant-garde musicians Cecil Taylor, Bill Dixon, and Don Cherry. By the time he recorded "Four for Trane" and "Fire Music" in the mid-sixties, Shepp had found his own voice in an idiom defined by John Coltrane, who became his mentor. Much of Shepp's music addressed the issue of race in America in a much more direct fashion than the majority of his peers. And unlike much art created with a social agenda, Shepp's recordings from that period are not dependent now on historical qualification. His playing was characterized by a gruff sound and a penchant for going "against the grain." The '70s and '80s found him integrating elements of earlier parts of Jazz's traditions into his music. Shepp's 1977 recording of spiritual themes (*Goin' Home*), made with pianist Horace Parlan, was both a surprise and a relevation to many in the Jazz world. A longtime teacher at the University of Massachusetts, Shepp's visibility on the Jazz scene has diminished. Most people hear him now through his recordings, where he has been addressing the Jazz tenor saxophone canon in a way that he never did as a young man, and the results have been intriguing.

Wayne Shorter (b. 1933): A distinctive stylist who came on the Jazz scene at a time when Sonny Rollins and John Coltrane were at the height of their powers and slowly created his own niche as a composer and as a tenor (and later soprano) saxophonist. Unwilling to follow the trend of "blowing sessions" that characterized so much of Jazz recording at the time, Shorter established himself as a thoughtful conceptualist ("Speak No Evil" and "Ju-Ju"). This led Miles Davis to hire him away from Art Blakey's band in late 1964. Shorter was the catalyst that turned this group into one of the most influential Jazz ensembles in the music's entire history. Possessing an uncanny intuition, they approached their repertoire with a composer's approach, stretching and bending the pieces to suit their needs ("E.S.P." and "Miles Smiles"). After leaving Davis in 1970 (shortly after making the legendary *Bitches Brew* album), Shorter, along with ex-Davis keyboardist Joe Zawinul, jumped directly into the budding world of fusion with the band Weather Report. Eschewing the acoustic aesthetic, this music was highly amplified and based on rhythms that had as much to do with funk and rock music as they did with Jazz. In its early days, there was a feeling of freshness in the band's output ("Weather Report" and "Heavy Weather"), but it lapsed into turgidity. Shorter remains a risk-taking improviser, with a highly chromatic and slippery style no matter what the context, whether it be reunions with his peers from the Miles Davis days in the group V.S.O.P (*The Quintet*), duets with Rachel Z. (*High Life*), or a rare acoustic outing with Jim Hall and Michel Petrucianni (*Power of Three*).

Martial Solal (b. 1927): A startlingly original voice in Jazz for over half a century, although largely unknown in the United States. Solal, born in Algeria, made his name in France in the 1950s as a tremendously versatile pianist who sounded equally comfortable recording with Sidney Bechet ("When a Soprano Meets a Piano") and grappling with the contemporary challenges posed by the music of Andre Hodier. Both his playing and compositions are marked by a penchant for compositional unity, a quality he shares with Ellington and John Lewis. Solal integrates influences from a broad range of inspirations, but they never have the effect of a hodgepodge, and he never plays by rote. He visited the United States on several occasions, even recording a live album at the Newport Jazz Festival, and has had a long and artistically fruitful association with Lee Konitz ("Four Keys"). Solal has also had a successful career as a film composer, and is currently involved in many different projects, including a recast tribute to Ellington that is typically challenging.

Art Tatum (1909–56): Though he died almost fifty years ago, Tatum remains unsurpassed as the complete Jazz pianist. It is astonishing that music as abstract and as rhythmically and harmonically challenging as Tatum's found a niche in the commercial world of his day. His combination of technical virtuosity was married to an abstract and frequently humorous style that led many to mistake the surface frills for its essence.

The secret of Tatum's appeal may very well reside in his melodic sense, for his solos are anchored to the melody in almost every measure, although he goes out of his way to obscure it in the filigree at times. Tatum was known as a solo pianist, and it was in that mode that he made his greatest recordings ("Aunt Hagar's Blues," "Willow Weep for Me," and "Get Happy"). Luckily, Tatum recorded prolifically from the mid-thirties on. He formed a trio in the early '40s, and although the results were intriguing, it hampered his freedom. There was also a series of sessions made with horn players in the '50s, the best of them being those with Ben Webster, whose economy of means made for a perfect contrast with Tatum. There was an informal side to Tatum that he revealed only in after-hours situations, and luckily some of those performances were recorded. Among the best are a pair of 1941 trio sides including the trumpeter Frankie Newton ("Sweet Georgia Brown" and "Lady Be Good"). His art was so complex and so demanding that it may be wise to listen to his performances a few at a time in order not to be overwhelmed.

Cecil Taylor (b. 1929): An idiosyncratic improviser who merged the musical worlds of Ellington and Monk with mid-twentieth century classical music in a fashion that remains challenging (to put it mildly) almost half a century later. Taylor was classically trained and has never felt the need to add more than the slightest smattering of what are considered the basic elements of Jazz to his highly charged and at times prolix music. His early associates included the saxophonists Steve Lacy and Archie Shepp, the bassist Buell Neidlinger, and the drummer Dennis Charles. Whereas Ornette Coleman, who appeared in New York a few years after Taylor, played music that was challenging but tangibly blues based, Taylor took his cues from the atonal stylings set in motion by Arnold Schoenberg and his own brand of pianistic hyperkinetics. His 1960 recording "The World of Cecil Taylor" is about as close to the mainstream as Taylor ever got and makes a good introduction to his always complex, frequently confrontational music. Alto saxophonist Jimmy Lyons played in Taylor's group from 1960 through his death in 1986, and added a tangible Jazz feeling to the proceedings. They made many recordings, of which "Unit Structures" and "Dark Unto Themselves" stand out. Many of Taylor's pieces, whether with his band, or in his longtime series of solo recitals, last an hour or more and demand an intense amount of concentration from the listener. Taylor was a founder of the Jazz Composers Guild in 1964, but generally found work hard to come by until the '70s. Since then, he has become an international attraction, playing solo piano, appearing with his variously sized groups (frequently integrating his poetry into the proceedings), and has played duos with Max Roach and Mary Lou Williams. There may be surface links to the Jazz tradition in Taylor—to Monk for the use of the piano as a purely percussive instrument at times, to Coltrane for the sheer length of the performances, and to Ellington for his staunch individualism—but his music remains truly beyond category.

Jack Teagarden (1905–64): The possessor of an extraordinarily limber trombone style, facilitated by an original method of economizing the movement of his slide that allowed tremendous flexibility. Raised in Texas, Teagarden was a devotee of the blues and singer Bessie Smith, and even played on her last recording session in 1933 ("Down in the Dumps" and "Give Me a Pig Foot"). His playing was at once laid-back, epigrammatic, and virtuosic. He also befriended Louis Armstrong at an early age, and later made many classic recordings and performances with him ("Knockin' a Jug," "Rockin' Chair," "Jack-Armstrong Blues," and "Stars Fell on Alabama"). While playing in Ben Pollack's band in New York during the late 1920s, Teagarden spent many hours jamming with two stars of the Fletcher Henderson band, Coleman Hawkins and the trombonist Jimmy Harrison, which was as about as sophisticated a musical duo as then existed in Jazz. He also made many classic sessions in the company of Benny Goodman ("Basin Street Blues" and "After You've Gone"), both of whom found great inspiration in the other. After an extended and frustrating stay in Paul Whiteman's orchestra, Teagarden led his own largely unsuccessful big band for seven years before spending 1947–51 as a member of Armstrong's All Stars. He spent the rest of his life touring the world with his own band, doing the occasional reunion with Armstrong and other peers, and recording. Among the highlights of these later years was *Think Well of Me*, a reflective and challenging set of Willard Robison's music.

Lennie Tristano (1919–78): A pianist/composer who was one of the most original voices in Jazz to follow the advent of Charlie Parker in the '40s. Inspired by the long-lined improvisations of Lester Young and Charlie Christian, Tristano sought to establish a new sound by emphasizing unusual rhythmic groupings and counterpoint that resulted in bitonal harmonic clashes that flew in the face of what was rapidly ossifying as the bop style. Tristano's disciples included the saxophonists Lee Konitz and Warne Marsh, and their 1949 collaborations ("Wow" and "Crosscurrent") retain their freshness after half a century. They also experimented with "free" Jazz playing ("Intuition") and in general sought to create without relying on bop's musical language. Tristano cultivated a cultish feeling among his musicians, and this led to a feeling of exclusivity that took them out of the mainstream of Jazz playing as the years went by. Nonetheless, his music was tremendously influential; musicians such as Bill Evans and Wayne Shorter found inspiration in the music's almost ascetic qualities. Throughout the '50s, Tristano continued to grow expressively as an artist, and his solo piano blues "Requiem" (a tribute to Charlie Parker) is remarkable for its blending of Tristano's idiosyncratic vocabulary with that of Parker's. By the '60s, he had receded almost totally from public performance and spent the last decades of his life teaching.

McCoy Tyner (b. 1938): A rare musician who is virtually unique among the innovators of Jazz piano in that he not only created an instantly recognizable style, but that he also changed the way that Jazz harmonies are played and understood. His early recordings with the Jazztet (*Meet the Jazztet*) reveal him to be well versed in the idiom of Hank Jones and Tommy Flanagan. Shortly thereafter, Tyner made a significant break with the tradition when he pioneered, to put it technically, the use of fourths during his epochal period in John Coltrane's Quartet (1960–65). Without delving too deeply into overtones and how chords are built, these fourths gave the music a more angular sound. Virtually all of Jazz harmony up to that point was built in thirds (the kind of chords most everyone learns to play on the piano). But when that basic interval is altered, the resulting chords not only sound different, but engender an entirely different set of vibrations from the piano itself. Tyner was not only a superb soloist, but was a master of accompaniment. He made many classic albums with Coltrane, including *A Love Supreme* and *Ballads*. It's worth noting that when commenting about figures of Tyner's (or Basie's or Bill Evans's or Teddy Wilson's) import, their influence goes beyond just pianists. Tyner has led his own groups—mostly trios (*Live at Sweet Basil*) and on occasion a big band (*The Turning Point*)—since the late '60s. Tyner's sound has evolved over the years: His touch has gotten progressively harder, his tone louder, and the musical rhetoric a tad bombastic at times, none of which, however, overshadows his stature as one of the true giants of the music. Among the highlights of his recent recordings are a duet with Bobby Hutcherson ("Manhattan Moods"), a session with Michael Brecker ("Infinity"), and a solo album of Jazz standards (*Jazz Roots*).

Sarah Vaughan (1924–90): Few vocalists in any genre have had the sheer range and expressive capabilities of Vaughan. Arriving on the scene a decade after Billie Holiday, Vaughan had none of the mannerisms or vocal quirks associated with Holiday or Armstrong. Her concept was a lush one, with the varied shadings of her exquisite instrument taking precedence over the acting of the lyric. This is not to say that her performances were devoid of drama—far from it. But the emotion came largely from the phrasing of the notes, and not from the words. And it was in this sense that she was a great Jazz instrumentalist and won the respect of her peers. Vaughan started out as a vocalist and second pianist with Earl Hines's big band, and it was here that she met up with fellow band mates Charlie Parker and Dizzy Gillespie. Though she was just turning twenty, she was able to grasp the melodic and harmonic implications of their burgeoning styles. Vaughan's 1944–45 recordings with them ("Mean to Me," "Interlude," and "Lover Man") created a new style of Jazz singing. By the early '50s, Vaughan gradually managed to maintain two careers. The first was as a pop singer, recording virtually anything thrown her way, backed by commercial orchestrations. The second, which established her legacy, favored elegant accompaniment by a trio or, on occasion, horn sections made up of superlative players. Two of her very best recording sessions featured great trumpeters—Miles Davis ("East of the Sun" and "It Might as Well Be Spring") and Clifford Brown ("Jim" and "Lullaby of Birdland"). Like virtually all other major Jazz figures, Vaughan lost her popular footing in the mid-sixties, and never recovered her former commercial stature. This left her free to devote her energies to Jazz, and she remained a regular presence on the Jazz circuit until her death.

Chick Webb (1909–39): The first great drummer/bandleader in Jazz. It wasn't until the last few years of Webb's short life that recording engineers figured out a way to record Jazz drummers, and consequently, the swing, taste, and sheer power of his playing was never truly captured on disc. But more than enough remains (mostly on broadcast recordings where he could play out more) to explain the extraordinarily high regard in which he was held. Webb established the Jazz drummer as bandleader and soloist, and set the stage for his disciples Gene Krupa and Buddy Rich, as well as Max Roach and Art Blakey. He formed his first bands in the late 1920s, and was resolutely anticommercial in the sense that he would only play music that pleased him. Webb's orchestra became the house band at Harlem's fabled Savoy Ballroom, where they thrilled the dancers and slew any number of bands in a series of legendary confrontations. Listen for the way he solos and sparks the band on "Liza," "Harlem Congo," and "Spinnin' the Webb." It wasn't until 1935, when his singer, Ella Fitzgerald, began her rise to stardom, that Webb changed his tune and began searching for the combination that would bring him a hit record. Vocals began to dominate the band's output, and they eventually struck gold with their 1938 recording of "A Tisket, A Tasket." Webb, who suffered from a spinal deformity all his life, died in 1939 and never received the sort of artistic recognition that would so clearly have come his way as Jazz became increasingly recognized as a fine art in the 1940s.

Mary Lou Williams (1910–81): A pianist and composer, Williams was, in the words of Duke Ellington, "perpetually contemporary." She earned her stripes in Andy Kirk's territory band of the early 1930s, and by the time they began recording for Decca Records in 1936, Williams was not only an adventurous and nimble pianist, but also an innovative composer/arranger ("Walkin' and Swingin,'" "Mary's Idea," and "Big Jim's

Blues"). After leaving Kirk in 1941, Williams led her own small bands, making a series of still hard-to-find sides for the Asch label in the mid-forties ("Stardust" and "Russian Lullaby"). Many top bands, including Ellington ("Trumpets No End") and Goodman ("Roll 'Em" and "Camel Hop") featured her arrangements, but Williams never achieved the commercial success that so many of her peers did. She did exert a significant influence, however, through her mentoring of many of the young lions of the time, including Thelonious Monk, Dizzy Gillespie, and Art Blakey. Her apartment became a salon for progressive musicians of the era. As the years went on, Williams became increasingly intrigued with astrology ("The Zodiac Suite") and the Roman Catholic Church ("Mary Lou's Mass"), and devoted years of service to the latter.

Teddy Wilson (1912–86): A primary influence on Jazz piano in the '30s and '40s, Wilson had an early association with Art Tatum, and the influence was reciprocal. Tatum may very well have learned about coherence from Wilson, while Tatum provided a lifetime's worth of inspiration from his sheer command of everything relating to the playing of the instrument. A master of spontaneous counterpoint, Wilson's elegant and Armstrong-inspired right-hand lines (he made his recording debut with Armstrong's band in 1933) set against a constant variety of counterlines in his left hand. He created an intimate and sensitive aura that was new to Jazz piano, where each and every note he played in both hands had a distinct purpose and musical responsibility. In addition, the way he organized his harmonic material presaged much of what most people thought was new in the music of Parker and Gillespie. Wilson played a vital role in two of the most important groups of 1930s Jazz recordings. As the leader of specially assembled studio dates, he used the best big-band players who happened to be in New York. Billie Holiday was frequently the vocalist, and these are the recordings that established her. The musicians included Roy Eldridge, Chu Berry, Benny Carter, Ben Webster, Cootie Williams, Johnny Hodges, Frankie Newton, Harry James, and Lester Young, and what they made of the opportunity to play together away from their regular jobs remains among the high points of recorded Jazz. Among the highlights are "I'll Never Be the Same," "If You Were Mine," "What a Little Moonlight Can Do," "This Year's Kisses," and "Just a Mood." Benny Goodman also appeared on some these dates and Wilson reciprocated by recording as a member of Goodman's trio. The tremendous artistic success of that collaboration led to the formation of the Goodman small groups as a working unit. This groundbreaking integration produced not only some of the most original and exciting music of the era ("Oh, Lady Be Good," "I'm a Ding-Dong Daddy," and "Dizzy Spells"), but broke down many of the racial walls that prevented black and white musicians from performing together in public. Wilson also played classical music. He was a pupil of harpsichordist Yella Pessl, and played the *Bach Concerto in C minor for Two Harpsichords and Orchestra* with her at Town Hall in 1939. Though he tried his hand at leading a big band, and then worked consistently with his own trio for years, Wilson never achieved the fame that came to other Goodman alumni like Lionel Hampton, Gene Krupa, and Harry James, and the resulting disillusionment introduced an ever-increasing element of ennui into his music. Although he recorded prolifically for the rest of his life, the best Wilson comes from 1933–45.

Lester Young (1909–59): A trendsetter on the tenor saxophone, and one of Jazz's most influential musicians, Young's relaxed way of phrasing and original melodic conception changed the way the music was played from the late 1930s on. He evened out his rhythms and insisted on playing in a softly modulated musical voice no matter what the tempo. Younger musicians such as Charlie Parker, Miles Davis, Charlie Christian, and Lennie Tristano found this combination extremely attractive. Young came of musical age in and around New Orleans, and the bluesy and contrapuntal music he heard there shaped his flowing musical style. He eventually wound up in Kansas City in the early '30s, played with the best bands there, and came to New York in 1934 to join Fletcher Henderson, where his understated manner was not appreciated. It wasn't until a few years later when he reappeared in New York with the Basie band that his genius was given proper exposure. That exposure came from dozens of classic recordings with the band ("Taxi War Dance," "Lester Leaps In," and "Time Out"), and also with vocalist Billie Holiday ("Without Your Love," "Me, Myself and I," and "I Can't Get Started"), with whom Young shared a deep musical rapport. His stature in the music world led him to become a bandleader in late 1940, although his sensitive temperament made that proposition difficult for him. With the exception of a brief return to Basie and a hellish stint in the army, Young led his own band from then on when not touring with all-star groups. Some of his best recordings were made in tandem with pianists Nat "King" Cole ("Back to the Land" and "Indiana") and John Lewis ("Count Every Star" and "Undercover Girl Blues"). From the mid-fifties, his playing declined along with his health, though his mind stayed as sharp as a tack. You can hear that on an extraordinary, honest, and at times bitter interview he gave in Paris just weeks before his death (recently issued as part of *The Complete Lester Young Studio Sessions on Verve*).

SIX

The Music

Below is a listing of fifty exceptional performances meant to serve as an entrée to the careers of some of the music's most important creators. This is not a list of the fifty greatest recorded Jazz performances. There are just too many other selections that could have been made. Indeed, each selection seems to suggest at least three others equally deserving of inclusion—but that is the nature of the beast with lists such as these. Many of the entries represent an artist's early work, chosen so you can hear the musician at that moment of self-definition when he or she entered that rare group who significantly affected the music as it then existed.

It's hard to designate recent performances as "classic," because they have not been lingering around long enough to be judged in proper hindsight. Nonetheless, the list contains a handful of works from the last couple of decades that have survived many rounds of heavy repetition.

While not every single corner of Jazz is reflected here, there are more than enough musical threads audible to take you anyplace in the music. Each of these recordings succeeds on its own terms and will hopefully entice you to check out other works by the artists you encounter.

In the course of trying to translate these musical events into words, you might encounter descriptive terms that are new to you; it might be helpful to look for assistance to Chapter 8: The Language of Jazz.

Autumn Leaves, Cannonball Adderley: Miles Davis thought so much of alto saxophonist Adderley that he made an extraordinarily rare appearance as a sideman on Adderley's 1958 album *Somethin' Else.* The ability to hear Davis in a setting other than that of his own groundbreaking band of the time (which included Adderley and John Coltrane) is instructive. In a sense, his individuality is thrown into even greater relief since he can't rely on the reflexive backing of his longtime rhythm section. But the men Adderley hired were just as brilliant: pianist Hank Jones (his solo should be etched in stone somewhere), bassist Sam Jones, and drummer Art Blakey, who coalesce into one of the great units of all time on this unique gathering. Adderley plays with great gusto on this piece, and his solo has all the hallmarks of a classic (as does everything here); it only gets better with repeated hearings. Thought of first as the replacement for the recently departed Charlie Parker, Adderley created his own niche in the Jazz world by virtue

of recordings such as this—first rate in every way and organized with a classicist's sense of proportion.

Bee Vamp, Eric Dolphy: By 1961, a reaction to what was perceived as a tremendous conformity in Jazz was well underway.
With reedman Eric Dolphy (who plays bass clarinet here) and
trumpeter Booker Little, we encounter two complementary
but divergent approaches to reassessing the vocabulary of Jazz.
Both had mastered the traditional modes of expression but
strove for new ways to assert their individuality. Listen for
the vocal tones they get on their instruments, and how they
swing no matter how extreme the content of their solos. The
rhythm section comprises three prime movers of the era: pianist Mal Waldron (who actually manages to exploit the out-
of-tune piano at The Five Spot, where this live recording was
made), bassist Richard Davis, and drummer Ed Blackwell (a
New Orleans native who had just recently come to New York
with Ornette Coleman's band). If you are really game, try and
follow the form of this challenging composition: ABACABA—
the A themes and C themes are eight measures each, and the
B themes are four. Even if you're not game, don't let the
complex form get in the way of experiencing this vital performance.

Black Bottom Stomp, Jelly Roll Morton: Here you have the
swirling polyphony of New Orleans organized with compositional genius by the pianist/composer Jelly Roll Morton. To
some, a front line of cornet, trumpet, and trombone would be
a limitation, but Morton gets more out of these three than

most arrangers do with a dozen horns. He also chose players who were masters at weaving New Orleans counterpoint, which is active but never cluttered. If you want to see exactly how creative Morton is, get out a pen (maybe a pencil would be more practical) and make a list of the different combinations of instruments that Morton uses, and how they keep switching. The backgrounds are always changing around (and there are the breaks, which he insisted were an essential element of Jazz), and note how he saves the big guns for the swinging out choruses. The advances in recording technology between this 1926 item and the tunes King Oliver's band recorded just three years earlier are tremendous. You can hear on this one what New Orleans rhythm sections actually sounded like at the time—and they're stomping.

Blue Horizon, Sidney Bechet: This 1944 slow blues is at times like a Jazz Bolero, building inexorably toward a shattering climax, though Bechet lets things wind down to a peaceful ending. No one performed with greater intensity and inherent drama than Bechet, who here plays his original instrument, the clarinet. His tone is impossibly big in all registers, and he knows exactly when to pace his modulations through the instrument's various registers. The content of each chorus is wedded to the characteristic tonal quality of each register he's in. This may not sound like any great achievement, but most players play their "licks" regardless of where on their instruments they happen to be; not Bechet. The other instruments stay largely in the background, providing a simple backdrop for Bechet to play off of (listen for the arco bass—it gives the band a fat foundation that a pizzicato bass doesn't). Of special note is the way Bechet stitches his solo together with just a few melodic motifs that never become tiresome. Much has been made over the years about Bechet's vibrato, the breadth of which some consider off-putting. I find it to be an indispensable attribute of his musical personality. Bechet's sheer eloquence is a poetic reflection of the myriad wonders that coalesced in New Orleans around the turn of the twentieth century and the young musicians who found expression for their genius in this truly American music.

Blue in Green, Miles Davis: For years it was thought that the musical pieces recorded at the legendary 1959 *Kind of Blue* sessions were one-take affairs—no rehearsing, stopping, or restarting. The unedited tapes made that day reveal that there was some talk, some incomplete performances, and more than one version of at least one of the pieces. But even though the material was new, the men in Davis's sextet were quiet studies. Audible throughout is the sheer spontaneity of the proceedings. With its chord sequence played at different rates of change depending on the soloist's preference, "Blue in Green" was quite unusual for its time. Pianist Bill Evans wrote the piece in response to a challenge of Davis's to come up with something based on two chords (specifically, G minor and A augmented). His impressionistic playing helps give this delicate performance its unique character. Also worth celebrating is John Coltrane's restrained tenor saxophone solo, coming from a time when he was giving in to longer and longer solos. After completing a rather expansive and convoluted solo, Coltrane apologized to the trumpeter, saying that once he started playing, he found it very difficult to wrap things up. Davis replied with something along the lines of "try taking the horn out of your mouth." No such admonitions were necessary this day.

Body and Soul, Coleman Hawkins: Popular culture during the years surrounding World War II produced many works of remarkable sophistication. This rhapsodic and harmonically adventurous variation on a well-known tune of the day contains only the briefest allusions to its melody, yet was quite a hit after its issue late in 1939. Hawkins had just returned to the States after five years in Europe, and many questioned whether he would be able to regain his former prominence as one of the leading improvisers of the day. These sixty-four measures took care of that. His solo was transcribed and published internationally in music magazines and learned by players of every instrument. Listen to the way Hawkins makes his instrument sing. He played the cello as a young man and had a lifelong passion for the music of Bach, and you can hear echoes of that throughout the twists and turns he so seamlessly improvises. Hawkins's accomplishment in claiming anything in the realm of art as his own is one of his greatest feats, and his approach to saxophone playing still exerts an influence to this day.

Boplicity, Miles Davis: While he was a member of alto saxophonist Charlie Parker's group in the late '40s, trumpeter Davis took great inspiration from Claude Thornhill's band. Known for their use of as many as six clarinets, French horn, and tuba, the band had a range of sound and dynamics that no other band could match, save Ellington's. These attributes were exploited brilliantly by the band's chief arranger, Gil Evans, who helped Davis invaluably in realizing his own orchestral idiom. The end result was a nine-piece band that had a short commercial life in 1948, but whose influence continues to the present. Listen for the way Evans blends the trumpet, trombone, alto and baritone saxophones, French horn, and tuba so that you are never sure exactly what the instrumental combinations are. They elide seamlessly, creating new and fresh sounds at every turn. The solos by Davis, baritone saxophonist Gerry Mulligan, and pianist John Lewis are spare, making perfect use of the space and backgrounds afforded by Evans. This is not just an arrangement, but an instrumental composition that is comparable in its originality of concept and artistry of orchestration to Ellington. Also demanding attention in its subtle way is the superb orchestral drumming of Kenny Clarke, which sounds as fresh today as it did in 1949.

Bye, Bye, Blackbird, Miles Davis: It's hard to think of another piece that better demonstrates what Miles Davis brought to Jazz than this 1956 recasting of what was by then a hoary standard. Following a relaxed tempo inspired by singer/pianist Bobby Short, Davis's patented muted tone, with its canny use of the microphone and the concomitant overtones, enabled the trumpeter to find a different voice than that of his open horn. Listen for how the rhythm section of pianist Red Garland, bassist Paul Chambers, and drummer Philly Joe Jones expands and contracts the beat by switching from the "two" of the opening chorus to the "four" of the solo sections. They created a standard for the era with any number of devices that they could almost telepathically communicate to each other to enhance the soloist they were backing. We also hear one of Garland's famous block-chord solos. An essential component in the sound of this band was the brilliant improvising and searching sound of tenor saxophonist John Coltrane, which provided the same contrast with the far sparer Davis that Davis had in turn provided for Charlie Parker.

Cubano Be/Cubano Bop, Dizzy Gillespie: Gillespie's 1947 amalgamation of Afro-Cuban music and Jazz was a welcome refutation of all the pseudo-African genre pieces that so trivialized what was in fact an important musical relationship. Much of Jazz's defining rhythmic sophistication stems from the influence of African and pan-African sources. In the midforties, Gillespie hired the Cuban percussionist Chano Pozo and devised ways to meld his incantatory solos into a Jazz context. One of the best of these efforts is this two-parted composition, coauthored by Gillespie and George Russell. It would be a while before what became known as Latin Jazz coalesced into a discrete genre, but there is an authenticity in Pozo's segment (at the beginning of the second part) that points unerringly to the future.

Fifty-Seven Varieties, Earl Hines: No sooner had stride piano become codified in the mid-twenties through the work of James P. Johnson than Earl Hines blew the whole thing to smithereens in 1928 with recordings such as this. Made just months after his historic collaborations with Louis Armstrong (including "West End Blues" and the duet "Weatherbird"), Hines did to the conventions of Jazz piano what Picasso had done to representational painting. He made us understand the relationships between melody, harmony, and rhythm in new ways with his startling juxtapositions. There are passages here which, if isolated, would be as hard to parse as a corner of a pointillistic painting, but their function becomes clear when heard as part of the total piece. Hines manages to simultaneously carry on two separate planes of improvisation. The lead passes from one hand to the other with no preparation, and there are even moments when one of them has to wait for the other to finish an idea before continuing. The narrative comes perilously close to incoherence at times, but in Hines's conception, this becomes an expressive device. If you can manage to hear this in the context of its time, the word "modern" as it is used in relation to Jazz becomes meaningless.

Fontessa, Modern Jazz Quartet: Pianist John Lewis made a close study of European classical music (most notably Bach) early in his career. He took the lessons he learned and adapted them to the blues and Jazz that were at the root of his musical identity. He had little use for the melody-solos-melody format that continues to define the great majority of Jazz performances, and employed it sparingly. This extended composition reveals his preference for a well-ordered sequence of musical events. It is based on a very simple set of motifs, which are then developed in a compelling set of variations. With only three other instrumentalists—vibraphonist Milt Jackson, bassist Percy Heath, and drummer Connie Kay—Lewis was somehow able to deploy these spare resources without the slightest sense of limitation. This was because each of them was not only a gifted soloist (Jackson was truly brilliant), but an equally superlative ensemble player. Notice how Lewis uses the standard walking bass and drum accompaniment sparingly, and the tremendously subtle touch Kay has on the drums. This also happens to be one of the best recording balances ever achieved and is a sobering reminder that with all our digital technology, these analog recordings from 1956 have yet to be surpassed. Listen for the strange section during the extended cymbal solo when everything seems to be recapitulating in reverse. This piece catches one of Jazz's greatest ensembles at an early zenith in its long career.

Foolish Man Blues, Bessie Smith: This plaintive blues captures the Bessie Smith that black audiences around the country knew so well during the '20s and '30s (she rarely sang for white folks). She was renowned for her ability to completely mesmerize an audience with her incantatory singing; just the sound of her voice tells as much of this story as the words do. The accompaniment is just right; sometimes the better-known Jazz artists she encountered on recording sessions took too much attention away from her singing. The trumpeter Tommy Ladnier blends in with Fletcher Henderson's piano and June Cole's tuba to form a perfect backdrop for her 1927 foray into what would today be called gender studies, but back then was just a commonplace of day-to-day information.

Gingerbread Boy, Miles Davis: Jimmy Heath's straight-ahead blues is treated to a radical transformation courtesy of the groundbreaking Miles Davis Quintet of 1966. Davis hired four men, each of whom became a leader in his own right and whose influence is still felt to this day. Each was also a superb composer, and developed a mode of improvising where any aspect of the material at hand could be isolated and made the subject of a solo. Listen, for example, to how tenor saxophonist Wayne Shorter takes the upward glissando from the end of the melody and works it into the fabric of his improvisation. Pianist Herbie Hancock was unusual in that he was more than willing to lay out when he felt the music did not need him. There is no piano behind the solos of trumpeter Davis or Shorter. Ron Carter on bass and drummer Tony Williams pick up the slack with an accompaniment that bounces on and off the standard blues form. Hancock uses only his right hand for his long, rolling solo, emphasizing the hornlike nature of his lines. These players took incredible risks with the material they played, and the lesson that subsequent generations learned from them had less to do with the specific stylistic quirks than the philosophy that guided it.

Haitian Fight Song, Charles Mingus: Like Jelly Roll Morton, John Lewis, and Duke Ellington, Charles Mingus did not need a large ensemble to express his musical vision. Here, he uses trombonist Jimmy Knepper and alto saxophonist Shafi Hadi in the front line. Mingus was a virtuoso bassist who stayed as far away as he could from the clichés that other bassists played. He starts this roiling piece off with an extended, vocally inflected a cappella unaccompanied introduction and then sets up a hypnotic mood with an ostinato figure. Everything about this piece flies in the face of the Jazz conventions of 1957. There is ensemble improvisation, meter changes, shouting (from the leader), and the wild, fresh feeling that Mingus always desired. He would actually stop a tune if he felt that one of his soloists was playing too many clichés. That is certainly not the case here. Knepper's solo is a masterpiece of melodic construction, and his playing was a welcome break from the slew of J. J. Johnson clones who were then receiving the bulk of attention. But the excellence of the individual solos is not what Mingus's music is about. What it *is* about is the overall idiom. Repeated listening will reveal how all the parts here fit together into a unified whole. Mingus told writer Nat Hentoff that the piece could have also been called "Afro-American Fighting Song," and that "I can't play it right unless I'm thinking about prejudice and hate and persecution, and how unfair it is. There's sadness and cries in it, but also determination. And it usually ends with my feeling 'I told them! I hope somebody heard me.' "

The Hard Blues, Julius Hemphill: This wonderful 1992 piece gets right down to the vocal core of the blues and is played in a truly American choral fashion by an all-star, avant-garde saxophone sextet. Hemphill was a musician who had a human tone on the alto saxophone and a compelling way of both improvising and composing. Listen for the way that the tones of a given player will sometimes blend with and sometimes stand out individually against the others. Hemphill uses cacophony as an element of contrast, and while it may take some getting used to, there is a deep beauty underneath it all. There is also a very strong element of African-American church music here, transmuted—in the fashion following the innovations of Coltrane and Albert Ayler—into contemporary Jazz.

Headin' Out, Movin' In, Joe Lovano/Gunther Schuller: This challenging composition begins in what sounds like a state of chaos, which gradually modulates toward coherence, a melody, and a tenor saxophone solo. Of course, with a composer like Schuller, the fun comes from divining how he will tie things together, which he does patiently and with a solid sense of drama. In the 1950s, Schuller was one of the founding fathers of what he called the third stream—the combination of the best elements of Jazz and classical music into a new hybrid. At the time, it was a welcome antidote to the well-intentioned but ultimately condescending attitude that Leonard Bernstein and others from the classical world brought to Jazz. Third-stream music had a checkered career and never lived up to its promise, but it is not without accomplishment. This 1994 collaboration between Schuller and Lovano reveals its best aspects. Schuller is thoroughly grounded in the traditions of the academy, and also knows what makes Jazz work. The success of a piece such as this depends on the presence of a great improviser. The immensely talented Joe Lovano enables this piece to take off into the realm of the spontaneous, all framed by Schuller's imaginative and unusual structure. Keep an ear open for the contribution of Dave Taylor, famous for his bass-trombone work, but heard here to great effect playing tuba.

Hearinga, Muhal Richard Abrams: This challenging piece from 1989 reflects the ever shifting and eclectic tastes of its composer, pianist and musical master builder Muhal Richard Abrams. It is reminiscent of the way that Arnold Schoenberg conflated the symphonic world of Brahms in his first Chamber Symphony. What once took forty-five minutes and four movements could now occur in a quarter of the time. Once you get used to the brevity of Abrams's episodes and become familiar with the various themes, a coherent and, taken in context, relatively expansive musical narrative begins to unfold. Abrams excels in making the transitions from one section to another. The performance benefits greatly from the expert duo of drummer Andrew Cyrille and bassist Fred Hopkins, who manage the various metric hurdles with alacrity, swinging all the while. Note how the solos of trumpeter Jack Walrath, tenor saxophonist Patience Higgins, and the composer all meld into the overall concept and flow one into the other while retaining the feeling of spontaneity.

I Gotta Right to Sing the Blues, Louis Armstrong: If the early recordings of Armstrong trace his burgeoning velocity and virtuosity on the trumpet, this 1933 classic marks his turn toward making fewer notes do his bidding. Written by Harold Arlen, who was an avowed Jazz fan, this superior song is a perfect vehicle for Armstrong. Confronted with a melody that already swings as written, he is free to layer another level of rhythmic invention upon it during his vocal chorus, which leads up to a trumpet break that manages to swing incredibly, though it consists of only a single note. But it is the precise placement of that note, and the way Armstrong manipulates the pitch and vibrato that make it so magical. What follows is one of his greatest solos and one that you might try to sing along with. It's an exhilarating trip! You'll have a lot of fun with the long glissando he makes during the break midway through the chorus—he times it so he lands on the downbeat with no more time to spare. Again, singing along will help you realize how difficult these feats are. They will also become favorite melodies of yours—guaranteed. For a demonstration of how influential this recording was, listen to Billie Holiday's 1939 version of this same piece where she borrows a bit from Armstrong's vocal and a lot from his trumpet.

I Want to Talk About You, John Coltrane: Coltrane was always a masterful ballad player, and throughout the many turns his music took during his years of prominence (1955–67), he always maintained a collection of reflective, slow pieces that afforded him the opportunity to sing plaintively on his saxophone. There is more than one version of his playing this beautiful ballad during the early 1960s, but one from the 1963 *Afro-Blue Impressions* album, with its lyrical cadenza, is unique. Listen for how the rhythm section, with drummer Elvin Jones at the helm, navigates the beat, gradually widening it as Coltrane builds. With a bolerolike sense of pacing, Coltrane gradually modulates emotionally into a passionate assault on the song that somehow manages to maintain its essence as a romantic ballad even in the face of thousands and thousands of notes.

I'm Coming Virginia, Benny Carter: This 1938 recording features Benny Carter's innovative and tremendously influential concept of writing for a saxophone section. With understatement and great taste (and that's a key element), he uses a panoply of compositional devices in the short space of a few minutes. Carter's arrangement kicks things off with a relatively intricate paraphrase of the melody (which was quite well known at the time), and once you listen to it a few times, you will begin to hear how Carter actually has the saxophone section accompanying itself with little figures that comment on the lead line. The level of playing here is superlative, with Carter not only leading the section, but also playing the alto solo (the tenor spot is by the Frenchman Alix Combelle). Bix Beiderbecke had made a famous recording of this piece nine years earlier, and Carter refers to it halfway through his solo. Hearing Carter improvise in the middle of his own arrangement gives us a sublime example of Carter's genius, which excels in the juxtaposition of both the spontaneous and the premeditated. As if all this weren't enough, there is a definitive solo by guitarist Django Reinhardt, who proved beyond the shadow of a doubt that a Jazz innovator could spring from foreign soil.

Joy Spring, Max Roach/Clifford Brown: Jazz evolved at an incredible rate throughout the twentieth century, and the harmonic basis of this charmingly melodic tune would have been highly unusual just a decade earlier. It changes key in every one of its eight-bar sections, which certainly keeps the soloists on their toes. Trumpeter Clifford Brown had such a tremendous technique that he skirted the edge of prolixity on occasion, but not here. He plays with a series of sequences that bring to mind another master Jazz logician, Benny Carter. Indeed, one of the great pleasures of his solo and his trading with coleader drummer Max Roach (whose first big gig was with Carter's big band) is hearing how he edits himself down to the essentials. There is a conciseness about this inspired performance from 1954 that hearkens back to the earlier eras of Jazz, when recordings had a limit of slightly over three minutes, and players had to learn to express themselves succinctly. All of these players were raised on that music, and its lessons show. Like so many great Jazz works, this performance abounds in details that only reveal themselves upon repeated listening.

Jump Start, Wynton Marsalis: This suite, written in 1995 for choreographer Twyla Tharp, highlights some of Marsalis's greatest strengths. The compositions are at once tuneful and thoroughly contemporary. It's a shame that those terms seem to be antithetical in Jazz, but so much of recent Jazz seems to have lost what was once its main calling card: the melodic imperative. The ensemble playing (by a slightly smaller edition of the Lincoln Center Jazz Orchestra) sets a new standard for Jazz performance. One of this band's greatest assets is that it has steady personnel who work virtually all year long. This has led to an ensemble capability matched only by the great big bands of yesteryear. Marsalis's music transcends the artificially induced demarcations of "style" that tend to divide the Jazz world, by arriving naturally at a synthesis of the music's past and present that has an essentially inclusive feeling to it. Featured soloists include trumpeters Marcus Printup, trombonist Wycliffe Gordon (heard at his very best on the haunting "Root Groove"), clarinetist/tenor saxophonist Victor Goines, alto saxophonist Wess Anderson, and pianist Eric Reed. One of the most mind-bending moments comes when ex-Basie/Frank Sinatra trumpeter Harry "Sweets" Edison guests on "Jump"—it's like seeing Clark Gable appear in a Coen Brothers film, but it comes off brilliantly. Marsalis has forged his individual voice in playing, composition, and, equally significantly, orchestration. Every measure of this wonderful piece bears his musical signature.

Keep Off the Grass, James P. Johnson: This piece, recorded the same day in 1921 as the far more celebrated "Carolina Shout," catches the pianist at the absolute peak of his powers and is equally worthy of close study. More than anyone else, Johnson created the idiom out of which all Jazz piano evolved. He packs into a performance of just over three minutes dozens of pianistic devices that inspired a generation of players, including Count Basie, Fats Waller, Duke Ellington, Art Tatum, and Thelonious Monk. One of the subtle delights is the way Johnson weaves other rhythms over the basic stomp tempo. Try and tap your foot along with him and you'll feel these little bumps that make the music swing all that much harder. What is remarkable is that Johnson's compositional sense is so well formed that the piece doesn't feel crowded with too many ideas. But of all the marvels to be discovered here, none is more significant than the sheer joy Johnson communicates with the perpetual motion between his two hands. It sounds like he was having a ball and could have gone on forever, which we know from contemporary reports, he frequently did.

Liza, Paul Motian: This George and Ira Gershwin classic (written in 1929) has a long Jazz pedigree, including drummer/bandleader Chick Webb's classic 1938 recording. Paul Motian created another essential version fifty years later at a dangerously fast tempo. His quartet, with tenor saxophonist Joe Lovano, guitarist Bill Frisell, and bassist Charlie Haden, sounds eminently relaxed. Lovano's solo is a wonder; it is at once melodic and tremendously fleet, and Frisell reveals why he is the most original voice on his instrument of the last two decades. He uses distortion and a gaggle of electronic effects that are downright shocking to those unaccustomed to the work of Jimi Hendrix, but underneath it all is a mastery of Jazz's narrative structure passed on by Frisell's mentor, Jim Hall. But it is the drum solo that astonishes. Motian makes his drums talk (no, they do not say "Put me back in the case") and it is refreshing to hear a player who was already a master in the 50s continuing to develop across the decades. In this sense, Motian is like Coleman Hawkins, who, as Martin Williams wrote, was always in the process of reinventing himself.

The Man I Love, Miles Davis: Out of the helter-skelter virtuosity that defined so much Jazz following the advent of Charlie Parker and Dizzy Gillespie in the mid-forties came an equal and opposite reaction. Trumpeter Miles Davis had a passion for space in his music, and this version of a Gershwin classic is spartan compared to what had been the norm just a few years earlier. After vibraphonist Milt Jackson's introduction, Davis states the melody with his classic muted sound, sculpting the notes out of the air with great delicacy. Then the tempo is doubled, and a series of wonderfully melodic solos follow. The pièce de résistance is pianist Thelonious Monk's masterpiece of swing and comic timing. He feigns confusion with the double meter (remember that Monk had played for years with Coleman Hawkins, who had introduced the concept of playing this song in this fashion), and then miraculously "finds" his place precisely at the point during the bridge where the lyrics refer to someone finding someone. (Monk was known for his ironic and powerful sense of humor.) He then proceeds to pile it on like gangbusters, without a speck of the "difficulty" he had before. The bass and drum work of Percy Heath and Kenny Clarke (by then already members of the Modern Jazz Quartet) is at once tremendously propulsive and intense, yet played at a restrained dynamic level. Davis was just at the cusp of his ascent to Jazz immortality (his quintet with John Coltrane and the orchestral collaborations with Gil Evans were still on the horizon) when this recording was made on Christmas Eve 1954.

Opus 1/2, Benny Goodman: The Goodman small groups, among other things, pioneered a new way of playing fast tempos. While there were a handful of contemporary Jazz players who managed to keep their coherence at great speeds, Goodman's units made the tempos sound slower than they actually were. This came as a result of their tremendous technical abilities and the unhurried way they moved from one eighth note to the next. Drummer Dave Tough proved that less could be more, even in Jazz percussion, by virtue of a relatively spare style, amplified by his great psychic energy. Listen for his subtle cymbal clickings and the bass drum, and how he implies all sorts of rhythmic shifts without ever resorting to anything louder than a whisper (extraordinarily well recorded for 1938). Pianist Teddy Wilson's solo is typically wonderful, but equally astonishing is his accompaniment as he provides the group's harmonic grounding, with bass notes that sound as full and thick as a tuba. He could sustain two, and at times three, levels of counterpoint simultaneously, while never making the music sound complex or dense. Both Goodman and vibraphonist Lionel Hampton had the equally rare skill to keep a rein on their virtuosic techniques, and clearly inspired each other to greater heights. They also knew how to accompany each other—listen for the quiet but swinging backgrounds they get going.

Parker's Mood, Charlie Parker: This 1948 slow blues is one of Parker's most brilliant improvisations. Known for his disordered life and his superbly controlled music (for all his passion, Parker hardly ever lost his bearing when playing), which was based on supremely sophisticated rhythms and harmonies, Parker could improvise with the brilliance of a great composer, as he does throughout here. "Parker's Mood" is immediately recognizable by virtue of its heraldic introduction and coda, which were the idea of pianist John Lewis, whose spare accompaniment and terse solo are also among Jazz's high-water marks. Lewis liked to use his piano in an orchestral fashion, and when you listen to him behind Parker—sometimes following, sometimes leading, and often perched between the two—it sounds like a spontaneously improvising big band. Parker's solo has been imitated so often in the last half century that its sheer originality and inevitability can be taken for granted. Each phrase leads directly into the next with a never-ending quality of developing variation. Listen to the first four measures for a perfect example of a musical question and answer. One of the most delightful and subtle moments comes when Parker reenters after the piano solo and suggests a tempo twice as fast. Drummer Max Roach reacts with alacrity and taste, proving beyond a doubt that many of the canards about the obtrusiveness of modern Jazz drumming were just that. The piece ends with a dissonant piano chord that is resolved only by a lonely bass note so low that it was cut off of many previous versions of this performance; listen for it, it's a gem.

Past Present, Kenny Wheeler: This floating and reflective ballad is a perfect introduction to the music of Kenny Wheeler. After distinguishing himself as a top flight Jazzman in England during the '50s, Wheeler branched off into the new directions of Jazz in the '60s. Instead of jettisoning what he had learned up to that point, Wheeler (like fellow Englishman saxophonist Tony Coe) managed to integrate the best of his past into his contemporary explorations. His playing here has a freshness that has everything to do with being in the moment. Also in this 1996 recording, alto saxophonist Lee Konitz (who plays some beautiful, winding chromatic lines in the midst of a plaintive solo), guitarist Bill Frisell, and bassist Dave Holland captured an ethereal quality that is reminiscent in spirit of the classic 1938 Lester Young Kansas City Six sessions.

Port of Call, Cecil Taylor: It's instructive to listen to this after "Fifty-Seven Varieties" for the similarity of Hines's and Taylor's wild virtuosity, desire to walk a creative tightrope, and disassembling of previous conventions. Listen for the contrast between Taylor's left hand, which keeps us connected to the harmonies of the piece, and his right hand, which ranges far and wide, sometimes into what almost seems like a different piece altogether. The magic is in the way that Taylor manages to make it all hang together. The drummer is Dennis Charles and the bassist is Buell Neidlinger, who wrote of this 1961 performance: "Cecil is highly conscious of theatre. His compositions are organized by juxtaposing elements of different moods against each other like actors on a stage. Moreover, he has the ability to order these elements so that the entire piece moves from the very first note to the last in an inevitable way. 'Port of Call' is a good example of this. It is a little journey through another world. The colors are orange and brown. The mood (mode) is set by the first chord, and is dissipated by the last chord."

Ramblin', Ornette Coleman: This rolling, blues-inflected piece is a wonderful introduction to the music of the man who championed what was called free Jazz. In reality, there was no more or less freedom in Ornette Coleman's music than there was in that of any of the other Jazz greats. The clarinetist Pee Wee Russell, for instance, had a similar attitude toward chord changes within a different context, to be sure, but he felt no need to oblige them if they got in the way of his point. Part of Coleman's importance was that he emphasized different aspects of the music than had others. Listen for the perfect unison playing from Coleman and cornetist Don Cherry. Their mastery of intonation was such that they could veer off into microtones at will, which gave their music a unique quality. Coleman's keening sound is the perfect vehicle for his associative blues playing. It is clear that both he and Cherry are master storytellers and deeply understand the narrative structure of classic Jazz, even if their harmonic system lies outside of what was then the norm. Bassist Charlie

Haden and drummer Billy Higgins provide an incessantly swinging and varied pattern throughout. Like the early music of Charlie Parker, it is difficult in hindsight to hear what all the controversy was about when this selection was recorded in 1959.

Reflections, Sonny Rollins with Thelonious Monk: More than most Jazz artists, Monk built his music around melody. Just knowing the chords and spinning out harmonic variations was not enough for his challenging material; you had to deal with the melody. This, the last recorded pairing of Monk and one of his major disciples, tenor saxophonist Sonny Rollins, is from 1957. Rollins equals Monk's ability to stay tethered to the melody no matter how far afield he ranges during his solo. One of the great joys of this performance is following these two as they bat around an up-and-down melodic motif (which may very well be an allusion to Monk's most famous piece, "Round Midnight") throughout. Both men balanced their seriousness about the music with their deeply ironic sense of humor, which gave their playing an unusually broad range of emotions. You can clearly hear why Art Blakey was Monk's favorite drummer, as he uses an implied double time to underscore every feint that the two soloists make, always there to prod them to even greater heights.

Rosewood, Woody Shaw: As an improviser, composer, and band-leader, trumpeter Woody Shaw created some of the freshest music of the '70s and '80s. Indeed, the great majority of his pieces sound effortlessly contemporary today. This work, re-corded in late 1977, is relatively simple, but the arrangement (by pianist Onaje Allen Gumbs) and the solos it inspires are first rate. Shaw managed to do what only few can—to create in an idiom that was totally contemporary, but was equally accessible to the general public. Shaw did this by virtue of his noble tone and superior melodic sense. The "groove" aspect of this piece reflects its time—Shaw was up against the high tide of fusion and crossover music—but it never weighs things down; indeed, it stimulates the soloists. Unfortunately, Columbia has yet to reissue the album *Woody III*, which contains his best orchestral writing. For those who want to follow up on Shaw, I would recommend *The Complete CBS Studio Recordings of Woody Shaw* from Mosaic Records.

Serenade to a Shylock, Eddie Condon: This slow, medium blues, which later doubles up into a peppily swinging romp, introduces a handful of Jazz's most eloquent and original stylists. Clarinetist Pee Wee Russell, tenor saxophonist Bud Freeman, trombonist/vocalist Jack Teagarden, and cornetist Bobby Hackett all found a way to skirt the clichés of the day and came up with personal variations on Jazz's basic text, the blues. Listen here for their subtle melodic touches and the sensitive way that pianist Jess Stacy and drummer George Wettling react to them. In subsequent years, this genre, like many others, was frequently ossified, and it should be a great pleasure for those who have only heard the lesser, later version of this brand of Chicago Jazz to hear it captured here in all of its pristine 1938 glory.

Showboat Shuffle, Duke Ellington: Throughout his life, Ellington was fascinated by trains, and no wonder—he spent thousands upon thousands of hours crisscrossing the country on them. Sleeping or waking, one could not get away from the incessant rhythms of the tracks and the engine, and Ellington used this as creative fodder for many compositions. This relatively overlooked 1935 piece begins with a repeated rolling, motorlike figure that gets passed around the band. It's the first of a number of ideas that Ellington keeps going in one fashion or another, and it's great fun to follow them. A hallmark of Ellington's band was the miraculous way his men expressed their individuality when soloing, and then submerging their sounds into the ensemble when necessary. Among the most original players in the band featured here were alto saxophonist Johnny Hodges and the cornetist Rex Stewart, both of whom made sounds and invented melodies like no else. Listen for the way Ellington wrote for trombones toward the end of the piece—setting them off rhythmically against the rest of the band. One small slip and the whole effect would be ruined. Of course, they pull it off easily, illustrating the brilliant ensemble playing that was always an Ellingtonian trademark.

Shufflin' at the Hollywood, Lionel Hampton: This 1939 piece is an early, and one of the most engaging, recorded examples of the Jazz shuffle. Long one of the music's most infectious rhythmic patterns, it is usually beaten to death by repetition in a heavy-handed manner and rarely heard in such a pristine fashion as this. Vibraphonist Lionel Hampton and tenor saxophonist Chu Berry ride effortlessly over the rhythm section (drummer Cozy Cole, bassist Milt Hinton, and guitarist Allan

Reuss), which manages to sustain the shuffle with a feathery lightness throughout—no easy task at this tempo. The overall feeling here is one of restrained exuberance with a tinge of mystery to it. Berry plays creatively in a riff-oriented style that eventually became dumbed down by others into the honking R&B saxophone style. The searching piano solo is by Clyde Hart, who makes the most out of a series of unison and octave passages. Hampton recorded this all-star series during his years with Benny Goodman (1937–40), and along with the Teddy Wilson recordings of the same era, they are the definitive small-group items from that very fertile era.

Singin' the Blues, Bix Beiderbecke: Like some of the contemporary Armstrong recordings, this performance is etched so deeply into the Jazz vernacular that it is difficult to imagine how different it sounded at the time. Saxophonist Frank Trumbauer (a.k.a "Tram") and cornetist Beiderbecke created a pair of solos that offered the first viable alternative to Armstrong's overwhelming genius. They had their own way of shaping their phrases, and threw the emphasis on different corners of the harmony. Out of this sprang a new melodic vocabulary that was tremendously influential. Among those who knew this recording intimately were Lester Young, Rex Stewart, Artie Shaw, and Benny Carter. Less remarked upon is the guitar work of Eddie Lang, whose counterpoint must have been a great inspiration to Bix and Tram. His function here is mostly in the background, but his nonstop commentary is an essential element in the piece's success. There was no precedent for this kind of Jazz playing in 1927.

Sometimes I'm Happy, Dizzy Gillespie/Roy Eldridge: This is a rare opportunity to hear two of the prime innovators in Jazz trumpet side by side during a period when all the elements of their styles were in perfect balance. Gillespie, by his own admission, had begun his career as an Eldridge imitator, and it is a tribute to his own individuality that there is no mistaking one for the other here. Roy (using a metallic mute known as a Harmon) introduces the melody, with Dizzy playing the obbligato in a cup mute, which is made of plastic. Dizzy takes over for the second eight bars, with Roy playing backup, and then they go back to the original formation for the rest of the chorus. The first solo is Dizzy's, whose playing has a reserved quality to it, while Roy's is more overtly passionate and heated. You can hear them challenge each other at times—sometimes they respond and other times they just let it pass. Indeed, the sense of timing and the amount of space they leave between phrases as they pass the melodic ball back and forth are as much fun to listen to as the actual notes they play. Dizzy's ascendance in the mid-forties had eclipsed Eldridge's decade-long dominance, and it was just as this recording was made in 1954 that Miles Davis did the same to Dizzy.

Steak Face, Louis Armstrong: One of Jazz's greatest pairings was that of Louis Armstrong and his favorite drummer, Big Sid Catlett. This is a concert recording made at Boston's Symphony Hall in 1947, and the venue's legendary acoustics helped to create a unique document of the way Catlett sounded in person. He makes his drum kit speak like the entire percussion section of a symphony orchestra, and he tailors his accompaniment to fit the style of each particular soloist. There are a handful of blues choruses by Armstrong (who floats way over the beat, leaving plenty of space for Catlett to fill with a panoply of punctuations, ranging from the explosive to the barely uttered), trombonist Jack Teagarden, pianist Dick Cary, and clarinetist Barney Bigard before Catlett launches into an extended drum solo. It is supremely musical and melodic and has no battering or bashing. Catlett was a superb showman, and while we cannot see what broke the audience up, every stroke makes eminent musical sense. And above all, the swing and sense of discovery that Catlett fosters in both solo and accompaniment is one of the marvels of Jazz's heritage.

Stompin' at the Savoy, Charlie Christian: This is a rare example of Jazz history actually being made and amazingly being captured by portable recording equipment. Guitarist Christian spent many fabled evenings of his all-too-short major-league career jamming to his heart's content in Harlem after finishing work downtown with Benny Goodman's band. Luckily, an undergraduate from Columbia University named Jerry Newman befriended a number of the young musicians who were actively involved in finding a new sound. Among the most prominent were drummer Kenny Clarke and pianist Thelonious Monk, who can be heard along with Christian here. The leader of the band was the trumpeter Joe Guy, who plays with a gritty intensity. Not restricted to the short solos allotted to him in the Goodman group, here we have an expansive and positively brilliant Christian in 1941, playing in a way that set the stage for Jazz guitar for the next several decades. One of the interesting facets of his style is the way he alternates simpler, blueslike melodies on the main part of the tune with much more exploratory and chromatic ideas in its middle section (the bridge). Greatly inspired by his mentor, Lester Young, Christian plays with a much more markedly even rhythm than was the norm at the time. This was one of the facets of his style that later captivated Lennie Tristano and his acolytes. Also of special note are Monk's fluid piano playing and the subtle yet aggressive nature of Clarke's drumming, and how they coalesce when Christian enters into a single rhythmic unit. Asked in later years why he never used a guitar in his bands, Monk answered that Charlie Christian had spoiled him for all other guitarists. This recording shows why.

Sweet Georgia Brown, Art Tatum: Recorded in Harlem in 1941 at an after-hours club, this extended performance finds pianist Art Tatum in a much more relaxed and overtly humorous mood than he usually was in the recording studio. He is joined by a bassist and trumpeter Frankie Newton, one of the unsung giants of the '30s and '40s. Gifted with a huge sound and an exceptional range of expressive devices, Newton's playing has a dense quality, full of detail and contrast. Although Tatum had the ability to be a superlative ensemble player, most times he chose to ride over anything and everyone in his way. What a pleasure it is, then, to hear him letting the music breathe and giving his band mates a fighting chance against his avalanche of pianisms. Listen for the unending series of harmonic substitutions Tatum unfurls over the song's basic harmonies, and how quickly Newton fields them. The trumpeter also wisely opts not to try to outdo Tatum. The best small-group recordings Tatum made were with men who gave him plenty of space, such as Newton and tenor saxophonist Ben Webster. The relaxed atmosphere of the club and its inhabitants is audible throughout and makes one realize the tremendous number of magic musical moments that were never captured. Thankfully, this one was.

The Tattooed Bride, Duke Ellington: Although improvisation is an essential element of Jazz, there have been composers who have been able to create Jazz masterpieces with next to none of it. This is one of Ellington's greatest and least known extended compositions and it is ingenious, constructed out of a handful of small motifs that reappear throughout the piece. Ellington was known for the humorous and frequently tongue-in-cheek stories he would tell in introducing his music. The one he used frequently for this piece had to do with a groom's discovery on his wedding night that his bride's body is covered with tattoos. These were represented by the short, back-and-forth squigglelike figures that comprise part of the opening melodies. You can follow these motifs throughout the piece and see how they lead into new tempos and keys. This is one of the most ingeniously structured of Ellington's shorter extended pieces. Written during the lean, difficult, big-band period of the late '40s, "The Tattooed Bride" was rarely if ever resurrected by Ellington in later years as were many of his other important pieces. And that's a shame, for it's one of his best. The most prominent solos are by trombonist Lawrence Brown and clarinetist Jimmy Hamilton (heard to great advantage in both ballad and swing tempos), who plays with a level of virtuosity that surpassed even that of his main inspiration, Benny Goodman, which is certainly saying something. The band's longtime drummer, Sonny Greer, paces this 1950 performance with great restraint. Indeed, this was his last commercial recording session with the band.

Tea for Two, Lester Young: This 1942 recording is radical from any standpoint. Lester Young and Count Basie shared a passion for letting their solos breathe, permitting the space between their phrases to define the shape of the music. This historic, but still lesser-known session (also featuring bassist Red Callender) pairs Young with the pianist Nat Cole—who had made a close study of Basie, Tatum, and Teddy Wilson on the way to forming his own innovative style. The interplay between Young and Cole is telepathic; they anticipate each other to the point that some phrases are merely suggested, but you get the feeling that they had been played in their entirety. (This sort of instant elision also plays a large role in the music of Tatum and Monk.) One of the many wonderful moments on this recording is the cat-and-mouse game the piano and saxophone play during the bass solo, and how their spare exchanges then slowly metamorphose into the full-fledged dialogue that concludes the performance. This was Lester Young's very first session as a leader and was made during an extended period in Los Angeles, during which time his band was appearing around town, at times backing Billie Holiday. It captures a unique moment in the evolution of his saxophone style from the pristine and airy music he made during the '30s to the more earthbound approach he developed in the '40s.

Time Out, Count Basie: When Count Basie's band made its first splash in 1937, many swing bands were in danger of becoming over-arranged and mechanistic. Fresh from years spent in and around the swinging provinces of Kansas City, Basie placed an emphasis on his loosely swinging rhythm section and a handful of brilliant soloists, who together created the sound of the band. In addition, the full horn sections were used in a spartan fashion and with great taste. Eddie Durham's "Time Out" is a wonderful example of the band's flowing and bluesy feel. After a brief statement from tenor saxophonist Herschel Evans, the band's main soloist, tenor man Lester Young launches into a Zenlike solo that makes a perfect complement to the spare backgrounds allotted him. Composer Durham plays the electric guitar solo (one of the first in Jazz) and Buck Clayton plays the tastefully muted trumpet. Basie's piano solo is definitive; he used quiet space like most other pianists used notes. It is the pauses between phrases that define the shape of his solos. The band's aesthetic is based on rhythmic flow, which stemmed from the lessons provided by bassist Walter Page. He was their guru, imparting his musical philosophy of how to keep the rhythm section and the horns in perfect concord. Page's ever-moving and well-chosen notes underpin the entire performance.

Twelfth Street Rag, Louis Armstrong: While there are many Hot Five recordings that are more celebrated, this 1927 item contains one of the most clear and profound examples of Armstrong's rhythmic genius on record. This well-known ragtime melody, often associated with silent movies and the like, was dated even by the time Armstrong made this recording. The introduction is a send-up, as are some of the licks the trombone plays. Try to tap your foot when Armstrong comes in with the melody; you will find it very difficult to stay on the beat. The space between the regular beat and the beat Armstrong feels is the purest demonstration of his rhythmic genius. It is the juxtaposition of those two beats that creates the swinging feeling. That's not even to mention the way he makes the piece sound like the blues or the way he wends his way through the diatonic harmonies with a genius the equal of any of the "masters" of any other musical genre you care to name.

Warming Up a Riff, Charlie Parker: Much of the best performance art occurs in rehearsal, when performers are creating for themselves and taking the kinds of chances not usually part of an official "performance." This 1945 recording captures Parker just minutes before committing his classic variations on "Cherokee," known as "KoKo," to disc. The tempo here is slower, and you can hear Dizzy Gillespie (playing piano) laughing and shouting encouragement to Parker, who plays in an expansive and humorous mood. This occurs right after Parker quotes "Cocktails for Two" and then transposes it to follow the song's harmonies. This was quite a momentous date for Parker, making his first session under his own name. It was also the first time that Miles Davis recorded with Parker, though he sits out on this track. The sheer joy in Parker's sound as he talks through his saxophone to his band mates affords us a glimpse of the happy Parker, and a welcome sound it is.

Well You Needn't, Thelonious Monk: This, coming from Monk's very first trio session in 1947, remains unsurpassed as a sample of his individuality. It consists of a rock-steady rhythmic sense; a quirky, personal piano technique and sound; a penchant for melodic variations; and an abstraction that equals Art Tatum's. Last but far from least, there is Monk's vital sense of humor with a large dollop of irony thrown in. This is one of Monk's less complex melodies and is based on two motives. (Acute listeners may note the rising tenor line that appears on some of the secondary A sections, and how Monk waits until the B section of his first solo chorus to reintroduce it.) Like Armstrong, Tatum, and Ellington, Monk was a master logician. Follow this piece from beginning to end to see how each idea flows into the next. Another highlight of this hard-swinging performance is the intense dialogue between Monk and drummer Art Blakey, which has a climax of sorts when Blakey hits a rim shot out in the open in the fourth measure of the last chorus. It's fun to hear this performance, first leading up to and then continuing from that one drum sound. Monk was one of the rare individuals who reinvents his instrument, and there is no moment in this inspired performance where the pianist could have been anyone but him.

West End Blues, Louis Armstrong: If there is one recording that represents the true genius of Louis Armstrong and what he brought to the world of music, this is it. By the time this was recorded in 1928, there had no doubt been many marvelous blues recordings, but Armstrong vastly expanded the genre's artistic boundaries. The introduction alone is one of the most famous moments in Jazz history, as Armstrong reinvents the blues, American music, and trumpet playing. Armstrong starts with a pair of arpeggios, after which the notes fly by in a blur leading up to the melody chorus. Should it come as any surprise that Armstrong plumbed the depths of his soul on a tune written by the man who changed his life, King Oliver? Every barrier—instrumental, linguistic, and metric—is transcended by the pure beauty of Armstrong's conception. With a gravely voice and a heraldic trumpet, he changed the world.

Who Wants Love? Lester Young and Billie Holiday: Although Billie Holiday and Lester Young became friends in 1934, it wasn't until three years later that they established a close musical relationship. But it wasn't until three years later when they were both members of Count Basie's band that it blossomed into one of Jazz's all-time great musical partnerships. As Lester himself put it, they sounded like "two of the same mind." On this 1937 classic, Young serves up a most relaxed introduction, after which he and Holiday engage in a constant give and take, passing the melodic ball around. Many times, musicians will accompany a singer by waiting for him or her to take a breath, and then filling in the empty space with a phrase or two. There is none of that here. Young spins a constant web of eloquent counterpoint around Holiday. Listen to her sing the tune, and how Young's melodies not only don't detract from what Holiday is doing, but actually enhance it. Then go back and focus on Young, and try to hear Holiday's voice as the background. During the last bridge, they switch roles, with the saxophonist crooning the melody in his upper register, which frees Holiday to paraphrase even further. The way they finally meet up at "in the air" is sublime. This is no more swing music than a beautiful Charlie Parker ballad is a bop piece. When you confront masterpieces on this elevated aesthetic level, they transcend such limiting groupings.

Without a Song, Sonny Rollins: Most people associate intricate arrangements with larger ensembles and a more freewheeling approach with small groups. The quartet that tenor saxophonist Rollins led with the guitarist Jim Hall in the early '60s made the best of both of these worlds. They alternated arranged portions with extended solo spots, and because of the highly thematic nature of their improvisations, always remained tethered to the piece at hand. Hall has blossomed in recent years as a composer, and it's interesting to listen to his playing here from that standpoint. Yes, he's improvising, but with an awareness of the piece as a whole, and not just as a collection of "hot" choruses. One of the most attractive facets of this 1962 performance is the way bassist Bob Cranshaw and drummer Ben Riley alternate between two and four beats to the measure. This gives the soloists more to play off of, and also creates a sense of variety. Rollins was one of the most eloquent improvisers to appear after Charlie Parker; indeed, when you hear Rollins introduce the melody, the sheer beauty and clarity bring to mind none other than Louis Armstrong.

Yvette, Cecil Brooks III: This beautiful ballad is presented in an unusual arrangement in which the legato melody is repeated throughout, with the soloists commenting over it. Drummer Brooks, whose tune this is, effects a long, gradual crescendo of intensity, carrying everyone along with him. This performance introduces some of the most distinguished young voices to appear on the scene in the '80s and '90s: trumpeter Terrell Stafford, saxophonists Justin Robinson and Craig Handy, pianist Geoff Keezer (who tosses in some thrilling octaves), and bassist Christian McBride, who were already mature improvisers and ensemble players when this was recorded in 1992.

SEVEN

Jazz on CD

The development of Jazz has been inextricably bound to recordings. Imagine if we could hear the way Beethoven played his own piano concertos, or how Shakespeare's plays sounded in their original Globe Theater productions. Well, you can have the Jazz equivalent when you listen to Louis Armstrong play "West End Blues," or Duke Ellington's recording of "Reminiscing in Tempo." Indeed, there are literally hundreds of classics to choose from.

In compiling a list of fifty top Jazz CDs, it would seem natural to recommend compilation sets that offer a wide array of the best recordings by different artists. But when dealing with the significant artists, chances are you will want to buy more of their recordings. So limit your compilations as much as you can, and buy complete albums by the artists you like. In the long run, you will be a lot better off with this approach and have only a minor amount of duplication in your collection. In some cases, these classics are no longer available as single albums, but have been folded into complete sets. This takes you into the province of large sets that naturally cost quite a bit, but are still less expensive than buying the original albums.

For those who have yet to buy one Jazz album and really feel the need to get their feet wet, the *Smithsonian Collection of Classic Jazz*, a five-CD set, remains the best general introduction. The brainchild of Martin Williams, one of the very best critics to assess Jazz, this set has both superlative selections and annotations.

There are many other classic albums by some of the artists mentioned here that many will feel should have been included, in addition to the many artists/albums that are not represented at all. That comes with the territory of trying to make any definitive list representing an artistic territory this large. So, acknowledging that it's a crapshoot in any case, it is hard to imagine that you will be unhappy with any of the recordings in this list, and if you are, they always make a nice gift, no matter what the intention!

Ahmad's Blues, Ahmad Jamal (Chess/GRP): The whiz-bang piano trios of Nat "King" Cole and Art Tatum in the 1940s established a tradition where the absence of a drummer was compensated for by riffs and notey solos passed between the piano, guitar, and bass. A decade later, the Chicago pianist Ahmad Jamal presented his take on that kind of trio and, in conjunction with bassist Israel Crosby and drummer Vernel Fournier, created a sound that took Count Basie's example to an extreme. Humor, understatement, and space became the defining characteristic of this innovative group, and its influence was felt all throughout the Jazz world. Miles Davis was so smitten that he "borrowed" and then recorded some of Jamal's arrangements. This 1958 live recording (made in Washington, D.C.) captures Jamal's trio at its peak with definitive performances of "A Gal in Calico" and "Surrey with the Fringe on Top."

Alone Together, Lee Konitz (Blue Note): Few Jazz artists have recorded as prolifically and for as long as alto saxophonist Konitz, which makes choosing a representative album difficult. This 1997 trio recording finds Konitz in inspired form: He has always been extraordinarily sensitive to his musical surroundings, and he was clearly getting the right signals from pianist Brad Mehldau and bassist Charlie Haden. There is much to be heard "between the lines" here, and what these instrumentalists choose not to play is just as significant as what they do play. In a Jazz age where more is frequently less, this sort of editing is indeed welcome.

American Pop: An Audio History from Minstrel to Mojo, on Record 1893–1956, Various (Music & Arts): What makes this nine-CD set essential is its broad context. By placing Jazz together with the other genres of music alongside which it evolved, the music's character is thrown more sharply into focus than it is in collections that segregate it from its larger environment. Virtually every nook and cranny of American vernacular music is represented here, from hillbilly to minstrel to military bands to rhythm and blues. Equally impressive is the quality of the transfers from the original recordings and the accompanying text, both done by the set's producer, Allen Lowe. This is a must-have for any serious student who wants to understand Jazz's true significance.

Baby Dodds, Baby Dodds (American Music): This fascinating 1946 document has the seminal New Orleans drummer (he recorded with King Oliver's Creole Jazz Band, Jelly Roll Morton's Red Hot Peppers, and Louis Armstrong's Hot Seven) playing, talking, and demonstrating his drum set. The extraordinary variety he extracted from his kit and the way he had it organized in his mind are important reminders of the craftsmanship, sophistication, and artistry that distinguished the first generation of musicians who defined Jazz. To hear him explain the function of the components of his instrument and then to make them all swing takes you back to the very roots of the music. It also sounds shockingly contemporary at times.

Bird and Diz, Charlie Parker (Polygram): This 1950 reunion is a fascinating document of the two most influential hornmen of their era. Charlie Parker and Dizzy Gillespie made a handful of recordings together in 1945, and shortly thereafter went their separate ways. Though they later shared the bandstand on the rare occasion and took part in an all-star, big-band date in 1949, this was their only subsequent appearance in the recording studio in their classic quintet formation. Both men were in inspired form, and although they only recorded four tunes that day, the various alternate takes and partial performances afford a fascinating insight into their improvisational genius. The rhythm section was certainly unusual. It would be hard to think of two more incompatible conceptions than those of drum virtuoso Buddy Rich and the idiosyncratic pianist/composer Thelonious Monk. But they merge in a wonderfully stark fashion, the common denominator being their superb time and mastery of the idiom. Two (of many) highlights: Parker's sincere and singing rendition of "My Melancholy Baby," and the way Gillespie turns a confused moment in the middle of "Relaxin' with Lee" into a primer on bitonality.

Blowin' the Blues Away, Horace Silver (Blue Note): Determined to bring large audiences back to Jazz in the mid-fifties, pianist Silver formed a quintet that played his tuneful and hard-swinging modern Jazz originals with the intensity and conciseness of a great Swing Era big band. As a pianist, Silver was a dynamo in both solo and accompaniment, and he is the engine that drives this band into regions of the sublime. This 1959 edition of Silver's band was one of his best, and it introduces two of his best-known compositions ("Sister Sadie" and "Peace") in definitive performances. It is virtually impossible not have both your feet and your brains engaged when listening to this infectiously groovy music.

Blue Interlude, Wynton Marsalis (Columbia): Marsalis's small-group recordings showcase his absolute mastery of making four horns sound as full and as varied in timbre as a big band. There are moments when it seems that there have to be at least five or six horns playing; it's fun to try and figure out who is playing what, and why it sounds so full. Maybe it was his exposure to the intricacies of counterpoint while playing all that wonderful classical trumpet music, or his devotion to Ellington and Jelly Roll Morton, or the music that came streaming out of his father's piano, or more than likely, some combination of the above added to the mysterious fount of all artistic inspiration that remains indefinable. Throughout this recording, the horns and the rhythm section are perpetually shifting gears, moving in and out of the foreground. The title track is a witty and innovative reflection on Ellington, while the other titles range all around the Jazz world (and other genres on occasion) in a refreshingly original fashion. Of special note is the reed playing of Todd Williams, who decided to leave the professional Jazz world shortly after this 1991 recording, and who was well on his way to becoming a major voice on his instrument.

Blues for the New Millennium, Marcus Roberts (Columbia): Pianist Roberts has had a distinguished career as a leader after leaving Wynton Marsalis's band in the mid-nineties. Usually heard with a trio, this recording, made in 1997, captured Roberts at the helm of a fiercely swinging thirteen-piece big band. It plays mostly Roberts originals, which, like his piano playing, are provocative and ultimately winning. You may want to try its version of Jelly Roll Morton's "Jungle Blues" for starters. Imagine what Duke Ellington's band must have sounded like to the uninitiated back in the 20s; Roberts's band captures that same spirit and freshness in the vernacular of today and introduces many new, top-flight players.

The Bridge, Sonny Rollins (Classic Compact Disc): This 1962 quartet date is one of the most structured albums Rollins recorded in his half century as a leader on disc, and also one of the most inspired and spontaneous. Guitarist Jim Hall, a perfect foil for the tenor saxophonist, was a rare musician who could parry and thrust with even the most extreme phrases that bounded out of Rollins's fertile mind. The repertoire is a mixture of standards and originals, with the version of "Lover Man" having a transcendent beauty. This is the kind of album you will come back to again and again, each time discovering new facets of brilliance.

Classic Sides 1926–1930, Jelly Roll Morton (JSP): Morton was Jazz's first great composer, and this box set gathers his greatest recordings. A superlative pianist, Morton managed to capture the free-flowing essence of New Orleans Jazz in his orchestrations. He used the best Jazzmen—many from New Orleans—and knew just the right context in which they would shine at their brightest. There are definitive moments from clarinetists Johnny Dodds and Barney Bigard, trumpeters George Mitchell and Henry "Red" Allen, and drummers Baby Dodds and Zutty Singleton. On the surface, performances such as "Grandpa's Spells" or "Black Bottom Stomp" seem like energetic, happy-time music, but underneath lies a labyrinth of compositional unity that will keep you engaged no matter how many times you return to these treasures of Americana.

Concert by the Sea, Erroll Garner (Columbia CK): Garner was what musicians call "a natural," meaning an unschooled artist—but only in the sense that his school was the bandstand, the radio, and the phonograph (where he studied assiduously)—who learned by doing everything one needs to know to become a great player. He was a force of nature: His music was relentlessly rhythmic and he played the piano as if it were a big band. Arriving on the music scene in the mid-forties, Garner's accessible and charismatic music was a boon to those who felt excluded by the intricacies of bop. This 1955 album—recorded in a converted Carmel, California church—caught Garner and his trio (including the legendary drummer Denzil Best) in peak form. I have never been able to put on the first track, "I'll Remember April," without having to sit down and listen to the entire album, so sample this one at your own peril!

Dance of the Octopus, Red Norvo (Hep): These rare recordings provide a unique glimpse into the experimental Jazz of 1933–36. Xylophonist Red Norvo was a gifted composer who wrote in a style that would three decades later be dubbed third stream. Norvo's pieces are clearly out of the genre Bix Beiderbecke pioneered with "In a Mist" (which gets a treatment here)—an amalgam of impressionism, blues, and the innovative chamber Jazz recordings Red Nichols made in the '20s. The earliest recordings on this CD, including the title piece, feature a chamber group that includes Benny Goodman on bass clarinet. The music remains startling and fresh as it veers back and forth between swing and rubato passages. Also included is a series of small Jazz band sessions that pair Norvo with peers such as pianist Teddy Wilson, trumpeter Bunny Berigan, tenor saxophonist Chu Berry, and trombonist Jack Jenney. All were to become major figures in just a few years' time, but here you can hear them while the fuzz was still on the peach.

Duke's Men: The Small Groups, Vol. 1, Duke Ellington (Columbia): Ellington is justly celebrated for his big-band work, leaving the equally brilliant and somewhat looser small-group recordings frequently overlooked. Though recorded (between 1934 and 1938) under the nominal leadership of trumpeter Cootie Williams, cornetist Rex Stewart, clarinetist Barney Bigard, and saxophonist Johnny Hodges, the music is pure Ellingtonia. Some of the titles were also recorded by the full band ("Caravan," "I Let a Song Go Out of My Heart," and "Pyramid") while many more are unique to this series ("Love in My Heart" and "Indigo Echoes"). There is something to marvel at in virtually every performance; these men had been playing together for so long and blended so well that sometimes you can't even tell which instruments are playing. Another bonus is Ellington's piano playing. In both solo and accompaniment he is never less than interesting, and often brilliant.

Ella in Rome: The Birthday Concert, Ella Fitzgerald (Verve): Most performers have at least a tinge of self-consciousness when they are recorded. Fitzgerald, by all accounts, was a nervous performer—not that you would know it from listening to the great majority of her work, but it was a factor when she recorded. Here she is caught live in front of a loving audience (she did not know the concert was being taped) in the middle of a 1958 European tour at the absolute peak of her powers. Though capable of startling shifts of register and timbre, one never gets the feeling that she is showing off. Fitzgerald's technique always served her art, which is far from common with virtuosi. The repertoire is first-rate, which was not always the case as the years went on. "I Loves You, Porgy" provides primary evidence that Fitzgerald could get way down inside of a song, a quality for which she is not always given credit. The accompanying trio, led by pianist Lou Levy, was clearly buoyed by her joie de vivre that evening, and the concert ends with Oscar Peterson's trio joining in for a celebratory jam.

European Concert, The Modern Jazz Quartet (Label M.): One of Jazz's greatest ensembles caught in rare form during a 1960 European tour. By this point, they were totally at ease with musical director John Lewis's challenging concepts. Their extraordinarily wide repertoire is well represented here, ranging from Lewis originals ("Django" and "Skating in Central Park") to creative interpretations of standards ("It Don't Mean a Thing" and "I Remember April") and two of vibraphonist Milt Jackson's definitive blues ("Bag's Groove" and "Bluesology"). All four members shine as a result of Lewis's insistence on a contrapuntal texture in which the piano, vibraphone, bass, and drums are always shifting between the foreground and the background.

Far East Suite, Duke Ellington (Bluebird/RCA): Ellington strove to produce extended works that reflected his status as an African American and that were not beholden to formal, European conventions. The "Far East Suite" comes from late in his career—1966—and is one of his greatest compositions.

It was inspired by a pair of extended tours. The first, made in the fall of 1963 for the U.S. State Department, took the band to the Near and Middle East: Ankara, Kabul, New Delhi, Ceylon, and other intriguing places that greatly inspired Ellington and his writing companion, Billy Strayhorn. The following year they went to Japan, which inspired the extended "Ad Lib on Nippon." They waited over a year before setting down to reflect on their impressions—Ellington wanted to make sure he had plenty of time to assimilate the influences—as the last thing he wanted to create was some faux exotica. All of the Ellington stalwarts are in inspired form, including the saxophonists Johnny Hodges, Harry Carney, and Paul Gonsalves; trombonist Lawrence Brown; and clarinetist Jimmy Hamilton.

Focus, Stan Getz (Verve): Tenor saxophonist Stan Getz had a phenomenal musical memory, a trait that held him in good stead when he made this very challenging recording in 1961. Composer/arranger Eddie Sauter, one of the most original voices in Jazz composition to appear in the wake of Duke Ellington, was asked by Getz to come up with an album's worth of material for saxophone and strings. Eschewing the usual conventions of the genre, Sauter created a series of vignettes for Getz to play with no preconceived melodies. Getz had to listen to what Sauter wrote and invent his own material, which brought out the very best in him.

Free for All, Art Blakey (Blue Note): This 1964 recording caught Blakey with a particularly fiery and creative sextet, which was no small feat considering that his past units featured Lee

Morgan, Clifford Brown, and Jackie McLean. Trumpeter Freddie Hubbard and tenor saxophonist Wayne Shorter were just on the cusp of becoming two of the most influential players of their instruments, and it is a thrill to hear them function in the cauldron of Blakey's beat. It is similarly exciting to hear how Blakey reacts to their very contemporary stylings. This band, which also included pianist Cedar Walton and trombonist Curtis Fuller, had been together for two and a half years (bassist Reggie Workman came aboard a year later) and had attained a remarkable ensemble unity. The title tune, a Shorter original, is the album's highlight. It starts out hot and keeps burning for over eleven minutes without ever veering toward hysteria or cant.

Further Definitions, Benny Carter (GRP/Impulse): Benny Carter has excelled in so many areas in Jazz that one would be hard pressed to name any single one as primary, but his innovative way of writing for saxophones may be at the top of the list. In 1961, he gathered his longtime associate Coleman Hawkins (they first played together in Fletcher Henderson's 1926 band), Phil Woods (a young alto saxophonist with whom he would record a pair of classic albums almost three decades later), and Thelonious Monk's tenorman Charlie Rouse. Carter wrote simple, yet stylish arrangements that brought out the best in each of these individualistic improvisers. They include one of the best renderings of "Body and Soul" that Hawkins made, and some of the most gorgeous saxophone section playing you will ever hear on "The Midnight Sun Will Never Set." The rhythm section was equally distinguished and varied: pianist Dick Katz, Nat "King" Cole's guitarist John Collins, bassist Jimmy Garrison from John Coltrane's quartet, and drummer Jo Jones of Count Basie fame. Also included in this reissue are tracks from a sequel album Carter recorded five years later.

The Goldberg Variations, Uri Caine (W&W): Adapting a classical masterpiece like Bach's Goldberg Variations to Jazz is fraught with danger. The original is so expertly constructed that something more than just improvised variations is demanded of the Jazz artist who decides to tackle it. In 2000, pianist Uri Caine pulled out all the compositional stops in this well-considered album that works fine whether or not you are familiar with Bach's original. He plays it relatively straight at times, contributing some elegant readings of the score, while not being the least inhibited about using the barest of musical relationships with the original to create his own musical universe. But that is precisely what Bach himself did with the theme that he centered the variations around; and in this sense, Caine is at once supremely conservative and supremely far-out, just like the great man himself. The supporting cast, which appears in many different guises, includes drummer Ralph Peterson, Jr., alto saxophonist Greg Osby (who sounds better here than on some of his own recordings), a couple of European String Quartets, and DJ Logic.

The Heliocentric Worlds of Sun Ra Vol. 1, Sun Ra (Calibre): Sun Ra made the theatrical element of his music so prominent that many in the Jazz world found it hard to take him or his band seriously. This was a big mistake. From the mid-fifties on, Sun Ra had a bracingly humorous and original take on the

Jazz tradition; he created his own frame of reference, and eschewed more and more of the musical common denominators linking most Jazz. It was a music that relied on ensemble textures and collective improvisation and an extraordinary array of instruments that had not yet found their way into Jazz. This 1965 album has a remarkable thematic unity to it. It relies heavily on the bass marimba and the saxophone solos of John Gilmore to thread the pieces together. Like an ingredient in a recipe that seems to be anomalous but serves to throw everything else into a new context, this album, with its own set of classic performances, may make you enjoy the music you already know all that much more.

Intuition, Lennie Tristano (Blue Note): There are few Jazz recordings from the late '40s that have retained as much of their freshness as these. The extraordinarily clean phrasing of saxophonists Lee Konitz and Warne Marsh (who were already well on their ways to becoming influential improvisers) helped give Tristano's music a surface sheen that could compete with the virtuosity that Charlie Parker's music of the era also demanded. But externals aside, what remains most significant about these seminal recordings is that they reflect a truly original mind and a group of players who learned a new mode of Jazz expression. Tristano eschewed cliché, and there are hardly any of the standard Jazz phrases of the day to be heard here. The program is varied—including Tristano originals ("Crosscurrent" and "Wow"), a standard that sounds like no other version ("Yesterdays"), and two early excursions into free improvisation ("Intuition" and "Digression"), a decade before Ornette Coleman. This reissue also includes a later session led by Marsh in the company of other Tristano acolytes.

Jazz Underground: Live at Smalls, Various (GRP): One of the best things to happen to Jazz in the '90s was the proliferation of young musicians who played night after night at an appropriately named club just blocks from the more famous Village Vanguard. This album captures some of the best of those bands in 1997. The music is refreshing for its lack of obeisance to the prevailing fashions of so much contemporary Jazz, whether it be the nth-variations on Coltrane's chord changes or long, modal vamps. All sorts of unusual and challenging influences float through these inspired performances. While some of the music has a slightly unfinished feel about it, that is by far preferable to so much of the prefab Jazz one often hears nowadays. Among the highlights are bassist Omer Avital's "Kentucky Girl" and "Hexophony" by pianist Jason Lindner's big band, and tenor saxophonist Charles Owens' "Scenic Roots."

Kansas City Sessions, Lester Young (GRP): Recorded in 1938 when the big bands were getting bigger and louder, a handful of men from Count Basie's band took the opposite tack to create some of the most quiet and poetic meditations on Jazz ever recorded. Three of the greatest minds of Kansas City Jazz collaborated in the making of this classic. Bassist Walter Page, who led one of the hottest bands of the late '20s, taught all of his sidemen invaluable lessons about pacing, structure, and, above all, swing. Electric guitarist and trombonist Eddie Durham was the first composer/arranger to capture the flow and spontaneity of Kansas City Jazz on paper. Tenor saxophonist and clarinetist Lester Young was the creator of a new aesthetic in Jazz that placed a primacy on understatement, rhythmic ingenuity, beauty, and humor. In addition to the four pieces (and four alternate takes) they recorded, there is another 1938 session featuring trumpeter Buck Clayton as well as a 1944 reunion that suffers only in comparison with the sublimity of the originals.

Keepin' Time, George Van Eps and Howard Alden (Concord Jazz): The acoustic guitar tradition in Jazz, if it is recalled at all, is usually associated with Count Basie's guitarist, Freddie Greene, revered for his metronomically swinging beat. But there was a handful of guitarists who created wonderfully virtuosic music in the '20s and '30s. The most famous were Eddie Lang, Dick McDonough, and Carl Kress, who were in awe of George Van Eps, who outlived them all. A master of the seven-string guitar, Van Eps was coaxed out of retirement by the young guitarist Howard Alden, and a series of four classic albums ensued. This, from 1994, is the last one, and has the feeling of musicians who are extremely comfortable in what was already an endangered idiom. Alden plays some quirkily beautiful Van Eps originals ("Kay's Fantasy" and "The Chant"), but the highlights remain the moments when both guitarists are playing together.

Kind of Blue, Miles Davis (Sony): This 1959 album is to many the definitive Jazz recording, even more than forty years after it was originally issued. While there is a tangibly reflective mood about the album as a whole, each of its fabled pieces makes for an effective contrast with the others. There is the relatively straight-ahead "Freddie Freeloader," with groove master Wynton Kelly playing the piano, while other selections feature pianist Bill Evans, and it was his brief but fertile period in the Davis Sextet that set off this experiment into new musical territory. Instead of playing songs comprised of many chords, Evans and Davis came up with a series of pieces based on much simpler principles. The effect on the other band members (saxophonists John Coltrane and Cannonball Adderley, bassist Paul Chambers, and drummer Jimmy Cobb) was galvanizing as they quickly adapted to the unusual challenge of dealing with material that was far less complex (on the surface) than what they usually played. But the quality that makes this album a perennial on the Jazz charts is the sheer poetry with which the band members interpret the material, and how well their variations wear decade after decade.

Lady Day: The Complete Billie Holiday on Columbia (1933–1944), Billie Holiday (Sony): These are some of the most joyous and lyrical Jazz performances of all time. Billie Holiday was a robust eighteen years old when we first hear her in 1933 singing "Your Mother's Son-in-Law" with Benny Goodman's band. Throughout the set she is accompanied by the greatest Jazz players of the era, including Lester Young, Teddy Wilson, Benny Carter, Roy Eldridge, and Ben Webster. They respected her as a peer (far from the norm for vocalists), and you can hear why. She manipulates timing, timbre, and notes just like they did, with the added bonus of having words at her disposal. The influence of Armstrong is everywhere: Hear it on both Holiday and Eldridge's "If You Were Mine"; Wilson's "I'll Never Be the Same" melody solo; virtually all of trumpeter Buck Clayton's work; and in the way Young uses it to find his own startlingly new voice on "I Can't Get Started" and "He Ain't Got Rhythm." But these are just a handful of the brilliant moments that permeate these sessions. The series ends in 1942, with Holiday on the verge of becoming the tragic, Edith Piaf–like figure of her later years. As this collection so clearly shows, that was only half the story.

Live at Carnegie Hall: 1938 Complete, Benny Goodman (Sony): It's hard to argue with Benny Goodman, who considered this the best recording his band ever made. Bands evolve in cycles, with personnel turnovers, new music, and public reception all playing a part. Goodman's band had been on a steady roll, both commercially and artistically, for three years. Goodman was such a superlative Jazz musician that few players could inspire him to play over his head. He had two in his band at this time—drummer Gene Krupa (who was to leave shortly thereafter) and trumpeter Harry James, and while they may have crossed the line of good taste on occasion, at their best they were galvanizing. A band is only as good as its weakest members, however, and this group had no "deadwood" as Benny used to put it. As an ensemble, the players brought a new kind of perfection and swing to their interpretations of the classic arrangements by Fletcher Henderson, Edgar Sampson, and Jimmy Mundy. But they weren't the only attraction that historic evening. There was ample room for the Goodman small groups, with Lionel Hampton and Teddy Wilson, and for a gaggle of guest stars including Count Basie and Lester Young ("Honeysuckle Rose"), Bobby Hackett ("I'm Coming Virginia"), and Cootie Williams and Johnny Hodges ("Blue Reverie"). The extended "Sing, Sing, Sing" has long been considered the definitive version, but for a more subtle and revealing moment, listen for the interplay between Goodman and pianist Jess Stacy during the clarinet solo on "One O'Clock Jump"—it's what Jazz is all about.

A Love Supreme, John Coltrane (Impulse! GRP): The last years of Coltrane's life (1965–67) were marked by an increasing agitation in his music that led at times to a purposeful in-coherence that turned away at least as many of his fans as it turned on. Given that context, the sheer songfulness and (rel-atively) straight-ahead flow of this seminal recording (made in December 1964) is all the more astonishing. Coltrane con-sidered this music his gift to God, which has made critical commentary difficult in some corners. But regardless of the extra-musical meanings Coltrane spells out in his liner notes, this music succeeds on purely musical terms. His quartet, with pianist McCoy Tyner, bassist Jimmy Garrison, and drummer Elvin Jones, had evolved into one of the truly definitive and innovative rhythm sections in the entire history of Jazz, and legendary recording engineer Rudy Van Gelder captured their empathic groove with clarity and sensitivity. This recording sold very well when it came out and has turned into one of the most popular Jazz albums of all time. It influenced count-less musicians both inside and outside of Jazz.

Miles Ahead, Miles Davis (Columbia): Unlike many artists who arrive at a concept and spend the rest of their lives honing it, Davis evolved radically from the very beginning of his career to the very end. Some didn't like where he went, but there can be no denying that he abhorred repeating himself. At his best, that reflex led him to create works of genius. This classic collaboration with the composer/arranger Gil Evans is both a highlight in Davis's career and in the evolution of the Jazz orchestra. Evans was a key voice in the Claude Thornhill band of the 1940s. The famous 1949–50 Davis Nonet (known later as the Birth of the Cool band) was an attempt to merge the sensitive aesthetic of the Thornhill band with Davis's burgeoning concept. This 1957 album, Davis's first for Columbia records, is a further and definitive expansion of that union. Evans's arrangements (they frequently veer closer to recomposition) create the perfect frame for Davis's intense sound and phrasing. On ballads such as "My Ship" and "The Maids of Cadiz," Davis soars over the ensemble like a great singer. The more uptempo pieces ("Springville" and the Ellington-esque "I Don't Wanna Be Kissed") show how Davis mixed understatement and a strong rhythmic feel to redefine Jazz trumpet. Evans intended the album to play as a suite, with each selection being bridged by a quiet note or two, and this recent reissue has restored that subtle but essential facet.

Music for Loving, Ben Webster (Verve): This deep and moving album from 1954 is a stunning success in a genre filled with mediocrity. To this day, the sound of a string section makes Jazz more palatable for a large segment of the population. The great majority of such efforts have been anything but artistic, and usually veer into the morass of "easy listening" or "smooth Jazz" categories. Here, you have one of Jazz's most eloquent improvisers and melody players backed by a string and woodwind ensemble arranged by Ralph Burns. Exquisitely recorded, this is a perfect marriage that brought out the best in all concerned. The pianists are simply the greatest—Teddy Wilson and Hank Jones—and they are spotted in short but telling solos throughout. The legendary Billy Strayhorn also played on and arranged four titles, including a rapturous version of his "Chelsea Bridge." Included as a bonus is a rare Burns with strings session featuring baritone saxophonist/bass clarinetist Harry Carney (like Webster, also of Ellington fame).

1937–41, Henry "Red" Allen and his Orchestra (Classics): The great New Orleans trumpeter is featured with three different types of ensembles, each of which highlights his asymmetric individuality and the high-wire nature of his improvisations. The first titles come from 1937 small-band dates comprised of sidemen from various bands. The fare is run-of-the-mill pop tunes done in the Teddy Wilson Swing Song format. The next session is a kind of updated 1940 New Orleans–styled all-star jam that includes drummer Zutty Singleton, pianist Lil Hardin Armstrong, trombonist Benny Morton, and clarinetist Edmond Hall. Though it may sound "traditional" to some today, their reinterpretation of four Crescent City classics (including Jelly Roll Morton's "King Porter Stomp") was as fresh then as Paul Motian's "On Broadway" series with Bill Frisell and Joe Lovano was fifty years later. But the real treats are the eight titles by the band Allen led in the early

'40s featuring trombonist J. C. Higginbotham, clarinetist Hall, and pianist Ken Kersey. This was a smart unit with crack arrangements and more than enough sophisticated turns of phrase to earn it a place in the pantheon of great small Jazz groups. Allen and Kersey play with such freedom that it's hard to think of the music of Gillespie and Parker, which took over a large part of Jazz just a few years later, as anything that much more "modern."

Now He Sings, Now He Sobs, Chick Corea (Blue Note): Corea has been such a major influence and a major player for so long that it is refreshing to go back to this, his first session as a leader, to hear how original his style sounded bounding out of the context of the 1960s. There were the influences common to the era (Evans, Tristano, and Monk) to be sure, but Corea's compositions and free-flowing concept set him apart from the pack even at this early date. This reissue combines the original album with other titles from the same session that were issued years later. Drummer Roy Haynes, who had already played with Bud Powell and Monk, demonstrates why so many great Jazz players have wanted to make music with him. Bassist Miroslav Vitous, just on the brink of becoming a major figure on his instrument in the fusion field, contributes mightily to the music when this was recorded in 1968. It was these performances of Corea's originals "Matrix" and "Windows" that established them as classics.

Percussion Bittersweet, Max Roach (Impulse): During the 1940s, Max Roach virtually reinvented Jazz drums, creating a new idiom in both accompaniment and soloing. His sound was crisp, he never bashed the drums, and he managed to juggle polyrhythms while making them swing. Unlike the great majority of his drummer/bandleaders, Roach was also a gifted composer, and this 1961 album may very well be his masterpiece. The compositions deal with many of the issues of the era. Roach achieved the elusive goal of making great art and making a political statement at the same time. Certainly this recording, with vital contributions by vocalist Abbey Lincoln, trumpeter Booker Little, and reedman Eric Dolphy, is anything but a period piece.

Point of Departure, Andrew Hill (Blue Note): This is truly timeless music in the sense that it straddles stylistic boundaries with naturalness and beauty that are anything but eclectic or self-conscious. Hill, as a composer and as a pianist, has a consistency of vision that makes his work all of a piece thus linking him with Monk, John Lewis, Herbie Nichols, Ellington, and Morton. What is equally astonishing is how Hill took a handful of players in 1964 with widely varied approaches—trumpeter Kenny Dorham, saxophonists Eric Dolphy (whose last studio date this is) and Joe Henderson, bassist Richard Davis, and drummer Tony Williams—and created a situation where they could be themselves, deal with some new and challenging material, and come up with a unified artistic whole.

Portrait of the Artist As a Young Man (1923–34), Louis Armstrong (Columbia/Legacy): The one problem with collecting Louis Armstrong recordings is that eventually you will want them all. Short of this Herculean task, this box set is the best place to start in assessing exactly how Armstrong redefined the music of the twentieth century. You hear him with King Oliver ("Chimes Blues"—his first recorded solo), Fletcher Henderson ("Naughty Man"), and Bessie Smith ("St. Louis Blues") on the way to making the epochal 1925–28 Hot Fives and Hot Sevens that showed the world how to swing. All of the titles, including a definitive sampling of the classics, are presented in excellent sound quality. For starters, program "West End Blues," "Stardust," "Weatherbird," or "Potato Head Blues" using the repeat mode. You'll soon hear how these recordings became basic equipment for living for generations of people around the world. Their grooves contain a reflection of the most profound aspects of humanity. There are also assorted oddities and rarities, including a 1929 appearance with Jimmie Rodgers ("Blue Yodel No. 9") and items from Armstrong's unusual 1934 Paris session, that add pieces to the jigsaw puzzle of his genius that would otherwise be missing.

A Portrait of Pee Wee, Pee Wee Russell (Dunhill, Fresh Sound): Though he was associated with the retro bands of Eddie Condon for decades, clarinetist Russell was one of the most forward-looking and provocative improvisers of Jazz's golden age. Never content to be bound by the harmonic conventions of the time, Russell, like Ornette Coleman and Louis Armstrong, found a way to "play the blues" over any kind of song. This superb 1958 session finds him in the inspired company of three like-minded individualists whose playing transcends simple categories. Trumpeter Ruby Braff, tenor saxophonist Bud Freeman, and trombonist Vic Dickenson managed to blend humor and beauty into a cohesive, swinging whole. They were also superb ensemble players; many of this album's best moments come when they play together, or follow one another in relatively (by today's overblown standards) brief solos that interlock like segments of a good crossword puzzle. The program consists of distinguished standards ("It All Depends on You," "If I Had You," and "That Old Feeling"), plus the pleasantly dissonant "Pee Wee's Blues."

The Procrastinator, Lee Morgan (Blue Note): Every so often a recording turns up that shatters your preconceptions about a player's style. By the time Lee Morgan made this session in 1967, he was well known for both his fiery technique and a series of high quality groove-oriented records such as *The Sidewinder* and *The Rumproller*. This album, which was released posthumously, is understated and devoid of any of the clichés that dot some of the trumpeter's other albums. Morgan developed into a composer of quality in mid-career. His pieces, which include the title track and "Soft Touch" and the two by Wayne Shorter ("Dear Sir" and "Rio"), are exceptional and inspire classic performances. The band comprises three-fifths of the Miles Davis Quintet (Shorter, Herbie Hancock, and Ron Carter) who were in the midst of recording another classic album, *Nefertiti*, along with vibraphonist Bobby Hutcherson and drummer Billy Higgins, who do some of their best work on this album.

Speak No Evil, Wayne Shorter (Blue Note): The early 1960s were a heady time for Jazz. Tenor saxophonist Wayne Shorter had arrived at a personal concept that reflected everything from his years with Art Blakey's hard-swinging band to his admiration for the more abstract stylings of Ornette Coleman and John Coltrane. Of the many classic albums he recorded in the period surrounding his epochal years with Miles Davis, this one from 1964 is widely conceded to be definitive. From Davis's band there is pianist Herbie Hancock and bassist Ron Carter. Coltrane's drummer, Elvin Jones, is also present, as is the fiery trumpeter Freddie Hubbard. The music sounds like anything but a mish-mash, as these fierce individuals fused into Shorter's challenging compositions to come up with a true classic. As Jazz writer Stanley Crouch has noted, the echoes of this recording still resound loudly in virtually every contemporary Jazz group.

Stringing the Blues, Joe Venuti and Eddie Lang (Koch): Many factors have contributed to the undeserved obscurity of these two early Jazz giants. One of the biggest may be the simple fact that they didn't play horns. But there is no denying the breathtakingly virtuosic musicianship, humor, and Jazz talent of violinist Joe Venuti and guitarist Eddie Lang. This dynamic duo made hundreds of recording sessions—as sidemen, as a duo, and as the coleaders of an experimental yet red-hot Jazz combo. The Dorsey Brothers (doubling on trumpets!), the blues guitarist Lonnie Johnson, and Bing Crosby all make appearances in this compilation (one session is reputed to have King Oliver on cornet, but the consensus is that it is really Tommy Dorsey). But the one musician who comes leaping right out of the grooves is the multiinstrumentalist Adrian Rollini. His booting bass saxophone is as limber as a clarinet, and yet anchors the music with great depth. This is a thrilling and rare glimpse into the white Jazz world sandwiching the 1929 stock market crash.

A Study in Frustration, Fletcher Henderson (Columbia): Henderson's band featured Louis Armstrong, Coleman Hawkins, Roy Eldridge, Benny Carter (all of whom are well represented in this collection), and many other Jazz giants very early in their careers. It gave them a high level of exposure on recordings that helped cement their reputations. His band evolved throughout the '20s into one of the greatest ensembles of the era, and virtually every stage of that development is captured in this two-CD set. The band could sound ragtag at times, and the title of this compilation refers partially to the feeling among his bandsmen that the group never recorded anywhere near its potential. That may have indeed been the case, but there are more than enough true classics here ("King Porter Stomp," "The Stampede," "Chinatown," "Queer Notions," and "Christopher Columbus") to make us very thankful for what we do have.

Thelonious Monk with John Coltrane, Thelonious Monk (Riverside): It is hard to single out one Thelonious Monk album since virtually all of his recordings are now available in complete sets and you may very well wind up buying them all in good time. Nonetheless, this 1957 item is a true highlight among the many of his career. Monk is at the helm of a fiery septet that includes Art Blakey and both Coleman Hawkins and John Coltrane in prime form ("Epistrophy"), and in a quartet featuring Coltrane (including a most tender version of "Ruby,

My Dear"). He plays an extended solo blues ("Functional") that reveals his stark, thematic mode of improvising. Every idea is intimately related to what came before, and you can almost hear Monk think as he constructs this lengthy blues epic. Monk reconciled a series of seemingly opposing philosophies into his music—dissonance and consonance; an original approach to the piano that sounds at once childlike and yet is tremendously complex; a strong, ironic sense of humor; and an honesty that is chilling at times. At the root of it all is a tremendous well of sheer beauty.

This Is Our Music, Ornette Coleman (WEA International): This 1960 album, the third release by Coleman's groundbreaking quartet, introduced the New Orleans drummer Ed Blackwell, who replaced Billy Higgins. Many found the straightforward title of this album preferable to the self-conscious ones that had preceded it (*The Shape of Jazz to Come* and *Change of the Century*). Among its many treasures is Gershwin's "Embraceable You," the only standard tune Coleman recorded during this phase of his career. It affords an excellent opportunity to get inside his head and understand how he heard the music that defined the conventions of the past. Coleman had a penchant for taking shapes from a tune's melodic contour and using them as repeated waystations throughout his performances. Listen for the shocking bass note at the end of "Embraceable You" to hear how this sounds in a relatively conventional context, and then look for the same effect through the other six of his originals, each of which is defined by a quirky, yet singable melody. Bassist Charlie Haden and trumpeter Don Cherry are indispensable components of this magical quartet. This version of "Beauty Is a Rare Thing," notable for its stark counterpoint, is one of the definitive performances of Coleman's long and distinguished career.

Tijuana Moods, Charles Mingus (Bluebird/RCA): As a bassist, composer, and bandleader, Charles Mingus abhorred clichés. This 1957 album features several outstanding originals ("Ysabel's Table Dance" and "Los Mariachis") that honor, but never merely ape, their south-of-the-border inspiration. There is also an outstanding version of "Flamingo" that is the equal of the famous 1941 Ellington/Strayhorn recording. Trombonist Jimmy Knepper, who did much music preparation, arranging, and composing for Mingus behind the scenes, is in superlative form, as are two obscure but sensitive musicians, the trumpeter Clarence Shaw and the pianist Bill Triglia. But the driving force is of course the leader, who does everything you can imagine and more with his bass, sometimes being the matador, and sometimes being the bull.

Time Out, Dave Brubeck (Sony): Although he was not the first to play Jazz in odd time signatures, Brubeck's tremendously popular band struck gold with this 1959 album that included the highly unlikely 5/4 hit, "Take Five." The group's sound was based on the interaction between the earnest drumming of Joe Morello, saxophonist Paul Desmond's whimsical lyricism, and the leader's original, if somewhat heavy-handed piano playing. They were capable of a wider range of moods than most Jazz bands, and their reflective version of Brubeck's "Strange Meadowlark" makes for a perfect contrast with some of the more intense pieces.

Tiptoe Tapdance, Hank Jones (Original Jazz Classics): Hank Jones is one of the greatest pianists of his generation. After listening closely to Art Tatum, he managed to extract the essence of his style without relying on a lot of flash and fireworks. George Shearing, John Lewis, Oscar Peterson, and Tommy Flanagan are just four pianists who admired and learned from Jones's example. This 1977–78 recording comprises six superior standards and three spirituals ("Lord, I Want to Be a Christian," "Love Divine, All Loves Surpassing," and "It's Me, Oh Lord"). The latter are notable for their freedom from any and all faux gospelization or hokeyness— they are, simply, deep meditations. In a music where rhythm is so vital, pianists have to have an extraordinary range of techniques to generate enough interest to sustain a program by themselves. Jones has taste and technique to spare, and there is none of the boredom or narcissistic virtuosity that mar all too many solo recitals.

20th Century Piano Genius, Art Tatum (Polygram): By all accounts, Art Tatum loved to play privately for friends. This two-CD set was recorded at the home of Ray Heindorf, Warner Brother's musical director. He kept a large piano in good repair and also had a first-rate recording machine. Tatum was clearly in good spirits and plays fascinating variations on his standard repertoire ("Tenderly," "There Will Never Be Another You," and "Yesterdays"). His attack on "Body and Soul" (the 1955 version—there is also one here from 1950) verges on brutal, as does his abstract sense of humor. There are also tunes that are unique in the Tatum discography, such as "Mr. Freddie Blues" and "Little Man, You've Had a Busy Day." This is Tatum in high gear.

Two More Pieces of the Puzzle, Woody Shaw (32 Jazz): A thoroughly contemporary and bracingly original trumpeter who appeared on the scene in the mid-sixties, Shaw dedicated himself to leading his own bands and had more than a modicum of success. His musical legacy is rich in variety and committed creativity, and this CD brings together two of his more adventurous recordings from 1976–77. One features Shaw's working quintet plus a few ringers, while the other is sort of an all-star summit meeting with reedman Anthony Braxton, Arthur Blythe, and a rhythm section that includes pianist Muhal Richard Abrams. What is astonishing is the consistently high level that Shaw maintains and how naturally he glides between the many admittedly challenging idioms.

Yam-Yam, Mark Turner (Criss Cross): Though he has since gone on to a major label contract and is now recognized as a major voice on the tenor saxophone, this first album from 1994 remains one of Turner's best. It is clear that he knows the idioms of John Coltrane and Warne Marsh inside out, and has listened to pretty much everything else that a young player should—but there is nothing precious, studied, or derivative about his playing. Joined by pianist Brad Mehldau and longtime musical companion/guitarist Kurt Rosenwinkel (another refreshing new voice), Turner turns in an imaginative reworking of John Coltrane's "Moment's Notice" and several originals, including a floating, medium-tempoed "Blues" where he and the guitarist seem to channel Lester Young directly into the new millennium. The other pieces have none of the self-conscious seriousness or lack of compositional merit that make so many Jazz originals boring. Turner has found a vital link between his writing and his playing that gives his music a feeling of maturity and of completeness.

You Gotta Pay the Band, Abbey Lincoln (Verve): To some, scat singing defines Jazz vocals, while to others it's anathema. Abbey Lincoln has never needed anything but the words of the song she is singing to get her point across. Like Billie Holiday, Ethel Waters, and Bessie Smith, Lincoln is a superb actress who portrays the complete range of emotions and associations suggested by the song she is singing. Never one to haphazardly program a recording, Lincoln approaches her albums, including this 1990 issue, as complete entities. She is also a gifted songwriter, and this version of her "Bird Alone" is a masterpiece, with sterling solos by pianist Hank Jones and tenor saxophonist Stan Getz, who play like angels.

EIGHT

The Language of Jazz

In the same way that it developed its own musical voice, Jazz has also spawned its own vocabulary. Many of the expressions that define American English from its mother tongue stem from the African-African community, and specifically from Jazz musicians. Louis Armstrong invented or played a large role in popularizing many of these. However, the great majority are not specifically musical, and therefore will not find their way into this glossary. Here we have several dozen terms that you will encounter in your reading about the music—many of which are largely self-explanatory, and others which need a bit of extra clarification.

From its beginning, most Jazz musicians used the same terminology as other vernacular, American musicians, with terms taken directly or adapted from European models. And as the number of players who receive formal training increases, the adaptation of terms is usually exaggerated and the old Jazz lingo becomes more scarce. Too often, the perception of a separate musical language of Jazz terminology is linked to some aspect of condescension toward the music or to latent racism or to just the plain old cultural inferiority complex that still plagues many American perceptions about American art forms.

A cappella: Performed with no accompaniment.

AABA: A common song form—usually thirty-two bars long, divided into four eight-bar segments—which consists of a musical theme (A), played twice, followed by a second theme (B), played once, followed by a return of the first theme.

Arco: In reference to a stringed instrument, played with a bow.

Arrangement: The reworking of a composition for a specific group or performer.

Atonal: Having no established key or tonal center.

Beat: The basic metrical unit of a piece of music; what you tap your foot to.

Bitonal: Played in two keys at once.

Blue note: A tone borrowed from a minor mode and used in a major key. The effect resonates aesthetically as well as musically, since the association with minor sounds is "sad," while the association with major sounds is "happy."

Blues: An African-American musical form whose standard length is twelve bars. In its early vocal form, it comprised a four-bar question, repeated, and a four-bar answer.

Boogie-woogie: A blues-oriented piano style characterized by rolling left-hand figures—wherein the left pinky plays the note first, answered by the left thumb—and repetitive riffs on the right hand.

Break: When the rhythm section stops playing, and an instrument or instruments fill in the gap.

Bridge: The B section of an AABA composition.

Cadenza: In a performance, a section in which the tempo stops and the soloist plays without accompaniment.

Changes: The chords that define the harmonic structure of a song.

Chorus: One time through a song form.

Chromatic: Incorporating notes from outside a basic key or tonality.

Comping: The accompaniment of a rhythm-section instrument to a solo—usually refers to the function of a chorded instrument (piano, guitar, or vibes), but can also apply to others.

Consonance: Musical sounds that feel resolved.

Counterpoint: The simultaneous occurrence of two distinct melodies; more broadly, a point of contrast.

Diatonic: Referring to the notes that occur in the basic major and minor scales of a given key.

Dissonance: Musical sounds that feel unresolved and suggest resolution.

Double time: A tempo double the standard rhythmic base of a piece.

Downbeat: The first beat of a measure; also, any rhythm that occurs on the beat.

Fake: To improvise.

Front line: The horn section of a band, usually associated with New Orleans music.

Gig: A musical engagement.

Glissando: The gliding up or down to a given "target" note, without clearly articulating the notes along the way.

Harmony: The confluence of two or more tones.

Head: The melody of a piece.

Head arrangement: An interpretation of a piece that is made up on the spot and not written down.

Horn: Any instrument played through a mouthpiece.

Laid back: Referring to a rhythmic feeling that lags slightly behind the actual metronomic placement of the beat; usually in contrast to "on top."

Lead: The primary melodic line of a composition.

Lead sheet: A musical manuscript containing the melody and harmony of a piece.

Legato: A way of phrasing notes wherein individual notes are not separately articulated.

Lick: A melodic phrase.

Melody: The succession of individual notes that define the primary shape of a composition.

Meter: The rhythmic base of a composition.

Mode: The seven scales that can be played on all the white notes of the piano, starting on one note and running up to the next octave.

Modulation: The change from one key or mode to another.

Motif: A musical unit that serves as the basis for composition through repetition and development.

Mute: An implement, usually wood, fiber, or metal, that is placed in the bell of an instrument to alter its tone.

Obbligato: A melody that accompanies the primary melody.

Off beat: A rhythm that is not placed on the downbeat.

On top: Referring to a rhythmic feeling that lines up with the metronomic placement of the beat; usually used in contrast to "laid back."

Ostinato: A repeated phrase, usually played in a lower register, that serves as accompaniment.

Out chorus: The final chorus of a Jazz performance.

Phrase: A melodic sequence that forms a complete unit.

Pizzicato: In reference to a stringed instrument, plucked with the fingers.

Polyrhythm: The simultaneous use of contrasting rhythmic patterns.

Real book: A collection of lead sheets.

Register: The specific range of a particular instrument or voice—usually high, medium, or low.

Rhythm: The feeling of motion in music, based on patterns of regularity or differentiation.

Rhythm section: Any combination of piano, guitar, bass vibes, and drums (or related instruments) whose basic role is to provide the accompaniment to a band.

Riff: A repeated, usually short, melodic phrase.

Rim shot: A beat struck by a drummer with a stick against the snare drum (commonly on the second and fourth beats of a measure).

Rubato: A musical device in which the soloist moves freely over a regularly stated tempo. The term has also come to be used to imply a temporary interruption of a piece's regular tempo.

Sideman: Musician hired by a bandleader.

Solo: An episode in which a musician departs from the ensemble and plays on his own.

Sotto voce: Quietly.

Staccato: Articulated in a manner whereby each note is separated.

Stomp: A swinging performance.

Straight ahead: Performed within the conventional Jazz format—4/4 time, theme-solos-theme, and an overall songlike structure.

Tag: An extended ending to a piece, usually four or eight measures, that repeats the closing cadence.

Tempo: The rate at which the beat is played.

Theme: The central melodic idea of a composition.

Timbre: The characteristic sound color of an instrument or a group of instruments.

Vamp: The section of a tune where the harmonies are repeated, usually as an introduction or an interlude.

Variation: The development of a theme.

Vibrato: The alteration of a tone's pitch, from slightly above that pitch to slightly below, usually used as an expressive device.

Voicing: The specific order in which a composer groups the notes of a chord; also, the assigning of these notes to particular instruments.

Resources for
Curious Listeners

It has long been a commonplace that words are a weak sub-
stitute for music, but short of putting many writers out of
work, there is something to be said for trying to explain, via
metaphor or just in a descriptive fashion, what it is about
these sounds that excites us. Here is a listing of books, magazines, websites, and film documentaries (on video and/or
DVD) that do the trick, and that come close to capturing what
the critic Whitney Balliett once called "the sound of surprise."

Books

Some of these books may be teetering on the edge of being
out of print. The websites Bookfinder (www.bookfinder.com)
and half.com are great places to find virtually any book you
are looking for.

American Popular Song: The Great Innovators, 1900-1950, Alec Wilder: This essential history covers the great songwriters of Broadway, Tin Pan Alley, and Hollywood. Their output intersected with, was profoundly influenced by, and in turn influenced, the African-American idioms that defined Jazz. Alec Wilder was an outstanding composer himself, and proves to be a patient and enlightened critic of a period that was truly a zenith in popular culture. Wilder traces the evolution of a few dozen major figures in great detail and goes out of his way to set things in the context of their times. The only glaring omission, fully in keeping with the author's sense of good form, is an appreciation of his own work.

Bebop and Nothingness: Jazz and Pop at the End of the Century, Francis Davis: Davis, known for his provocative essays in *The Atlantic Monthly,* is one of the best observers of the contemporary Jazz scene. Unlike many writers, he doesn't seem biased toward any of the music's "schools," and writes with insight and a very healthy sense of humor, which is refreshing. The way he deals with contemporary musicians may be his strongest suit—he takes them seriously enough to have fun with the music.

Beneath the Underdog, Charles Mingus: This autobiography reflects the man who wrote it: full of self-aggrandizement, genius, vulnerability, and humanity—a man who struggled to find a way to deal with the insanity of life in his times. There are segments of this book (which tells tall tales in the same way that Jelly Roll Morton did—only half expecting to be believed) that through their hyperbole tell us more about the topic at hand than any number of more sober, factual essays ever could. The Duke Ellington and Fats Navarro episodes alone are worth the price of admission.

Benny Carter: A Life in American Music, Morrie Berger, Edward Berger, and James Patrick (2nd edition): One of the most comprehensive studies ever devoted to a single Jazz artist, this two-volume work was hailed as a milestone of Jazz scholarship when it was first published in 1982. Carter's career is placed within the broader context of American social and musical life. The new edition sheds greater light on the reticent Carter's character and thoroughly updates the discography to include his extensive activities in the 1980s and '90s.

Bird's Diary, Ken Vail: Vail takes his subjects from the start of their professional careers (he has also done Billie Holiday, Miles Davis, and an overview of Jazz) and traces them as best he can day by day. Using an unusually broad range of sources, he constructs a narrative that gives the reader a tangible feeling for how these people actually experienced their lives. As important as the text are the photos and reproductions of material that flood every page.

Collected Works: A Journal of Jazz 1954–1999, Whitney Balliett: This collection covers Balliett's close to half a century as one of jazz's most influential and perceptive critics. He is at his best when writing profiles of musicians he admires. Like his fellow *New Yorker* writer Joseph Mitchell, Balliett has an extraordinary ear for the cadences and idiosyncrasies of his subject's speech patterns and weaves them into his own insightful prose, arriving at the literary equivalent not of a photograph, but of a painting.

Creole New Orleans: Race and Americanization, Arnold R. Hirsch and Joseph Logsdon, eds.: A thorough and at times fascinating collection of essays tracing the evolution of New Orleans from a French, then Spanish, colony to its Americanization. To really understand how jazz was created, an understanding of this history is essential. Jerah Johnson's essay on New Orleans's identity as a French society is especially original and provocative.

Don't the Moon Look Lonesome, Stanley Crouch: A sweeping novel that tells the story of a black saxophonist and his white singer girlfriend. Crouch, known primarily for his singular take on American culture, was a professional Jazz drummer before becoming a man of letters. He pulls out all of the stops in this fascinating tale of Americana, including many observations about what goes on on the Jazz bandstand that you will not find anywhere else.

Drummin' Men, Burt Korall: A definitive account of the evolution of Jazz drumming from New Orleans through the end of the Swing Era. Though most of them were thought by the public to be maniacs (Gene Krupa, who was in truth a superior drummer, represented to many the wild-eyed, rhythmically intoxicated drummer for decades), they were in general a thoughtful bunch. We discover that most of them were well aware of their significance in the creation of this fine art form. Thorough research led to the use of the best of what has been written and said about these great drummers— collated and amplified by the author, who plays enough drums himself to set things in the proper context.

The Duke Ellington Reader, Mark Tucker, ed.: A well considered compilation of much of the best material written by and about Ellington. There are many surprises to be found here, from the early appreciation of Ellington as a serious artist (from the late '20s) to a series of unusually frank articles and interviews that Ellington gave where he let his much vaunted guard down, even if only for a moment.

Early Jazz: Its Roots and Musical Development, Gunther Schuller: Simply put, this has been one of the definitive books on the music since its publication in the 1960s. Schuller brought all of his brilliance as a composer, conductor, educator, and instrumentalist to bear on the music from a historical and musical perspective. While some of his judgments (especially about the virtues of the post-twenties Armstrong) are questionable, the route he takes to these summations contain enough food for thought to stimulate any and all readers to draw their own conclusions.

His Eye Is on the Sparrow, Ethel Waters: This is one of the best Jazz autobiographies, for it captures the tone and cadence of its author. Waters had a childhood from hell, and it is recounted in great detail, yet with not even an iota of self-pity. She is brutally frank about her career, her romances, and the choices she made for herself at a time when most black women were stifled under any number of racial and cultural yokes. Waters was a seminal influence on Jazz singing and a pioneer in the integration of the American entertainment world, and this book takes you right to the center of her tumultuous and brave life.

In Search of Buddy Bolden, Donald Marquis: This fascinating investigation into the earliest roots of Jazz traces the life of ur-Jazzman Bolden. He came to fame at the turn of the twentieth century, and though he never recorded, the stories about both the man and the music were legion. After spending decades in a Louisiana insane asylum, Bolden died just as Louis Armstrong was becoming an international star. Marquis did an enormous amount of original research to separate the facts from the legend, and from it constructed a gripping narrative that is both captivating and good history.

In the Spirit of Jazz: The Otis Ferguson Reader, Dorothy Chamberlain and Robert Wilson, eds.: Ferguson was, along with Roger Pryor Dodge, one of the very first Americans to write intelligently about Jazz. Ferguson wrote for *The New Republic*, and while on staff there, he exchanged ideas with many of the finest writers of his generation, including Malcolm Cowley. He became friendly with Benny Goodman, John Hammond, Teddy Wilson, Red Norvo, and other leading lights of the music, wrote with great candor and prescience about their music, and was not in the least bit afraid of attacking sacred cows.

Jazz: A History of America's Music, Geoffrey C. Ward and Ken Burns: This large book is the companion to Ken Burns's *Jazz* documentary, and contains much material that never made it into the final televised script. It is as good an overview as exists of the entire music of the century, written in a fashion that makes it accessible to everyone. Ward is a first-rate popular historian, and his writing style is inclusive. In addition, this huge tome is crammed with photographs, many of them rare. There are also sidebars by a bevy of prominent authors.

The Jazz Life, Nat Hentoff: Known now for his persevering dedication to the First Amendment and all of its myriad social implications, Hentoff was one of the best Jazz journalists of the '50s and '60s. This book deals with the day-to-day existence of the much-vaunted Jazz giants of the mid-twentieth century, and is a vital reminder of the challenges they faced both on and off the bandstand. Musicians from Ellington to Mingus to Parker trusted Hentoff, and he actually listened to and learned from what they said. Though it was written several decades ago, this remains an essential read.

Jazz People, Dan Morgenstern and Ole Brask: Suffice it to say that Morgenstern is one of the best people to have ever written on Jazz, though the great majority of his work has been in the province of short pieces, essays, and liner notes. Here he is at his best, in long form, bringing to life many of Jazz's greatest figures in a seemingly informal fashion (no small feat, this) yet setting them in the proper context as the giants they truly are. His text is wrapped around the superb photographs by Brask. Morgenstern is one of the only Jazz writers who has been accepted over the years by the musicians as a peer, and his love and knowledge for the music and the musicians informs every paragraph.

A Jazz Retrospect, Max Harrison: Harrison was one of the first and remains one of the best writers with a strong background in classical music that shows absolutely no traces of condescension to Jazz. Indeed, he even condescends up to classical music (humorously) at times. This collection brings together short pieces written for *Jazz Monthly* and *Jazz Review* from the mid-fifties though the early '70s, and they have retained their bite and their relevance.

The Jazz Tradition, Martin Williams: This is one of the most essential books on the topic for the serious student, yet it is also eminently accessible for novices, too. Originally published in 1970, and revised twice (the last edition finished in 1992, shortly before Williams's death), Williams eschewed any and all of the conceits of the fan magazine mentality that had spawned much of Jazz criticism and that continued to trail it for so long. Williams's ideas have been extremely influential, and are aging very, very well.

John Coltrane: His Life and Music, Lewis Porter: Musicologist Porter is rare in that his intensely analytical purview can spawn a good read, and here he has come up with one of the best Jazz biographies to date. Through immense research and a passion for the details of the music, Porter blows away many of the cobwebs that frequently surround the lives of our vaunted Jazz giants, and emerges with a clear and concise narrative that is chock-full of musical examples (for those brave enough to try to play them!).

Kind of Blue, Ashley Kahn: This is the biography of a record album, and not just any album, but one that is touted as being the best-selling one of all time. Kahn found his way to the best sources (including the only surviving member of the 1959 Miles Davis band, Jimmy Cobb) and treads the line between musicology and journalism with élan. This compact book will please both the musician and the layman, and lead them both back to the music with more food for thought.

Living with Music: Ralph Ellison's Jazz Writings, Ralph Ellison, Robert G. O'Meally, ed.: Known for his searing novel *Invisible Man*, Ellison grew up in Oklahoma City, surrounded by the soon-to-be legends who defined Kansas City Swing. He heard Charlie Christian, Lester Young, Jimmy Rushing, and many others while he was making up his mind whether or not to become a professional musician. No one has ever surpassed his essays on Jazz and what it meant to the world in which it was created and how it related to the world that came after. Luckily, O'Meally, a disciple of Ellison's, has plucked these Jazz-related writings (which includes some previously unpublished items, including letters) and set them properly like the jewels they are.

Louis Armstrong, in His Own Words: Selected Writings, Louis Armstrong, Thomas David Brothers, ed.: Armstrong was a prolific writer who carried a portable typewriter with him wherever he traveled, and when that wasn't at hand, was not averse to writing long letters in his own hand. This collection collates the best examples from the voluminous archives that exist, and reveal a far more complex individual, which will shock those who only see the external mask of his stage persona. There are autobiographical sections, letters to his manager, and letters to his friends, all of which reflect a wise, at times canny, and, ultimately, quintessentially human being.

Music Is My Mistress, Duke Ellington: A long memoir actually written by the great man himself that reveals the many masks he wore during his long, and to many, invisible life. Invisible in the sense that very few saw him for what he truly was— one of the greatest composers America has ever produced and an extraordinary pianist. The famous bandleader/composer persona gets its due, though Ellington's take on it all displays many different truths coated with wit and irony. The core of this book is his reminiscences on favorite people, and journals of some of his foreign tours during his last decade.

Reading Jazz: A Gathering of Autobiography, Reportage, and Criticism from 1919 to Now, Robert Gottlieb, ed.: The title's "now" being just a few years ago, this large collection brings together the widest array of high quality writing on Jazz to date. This mammoth compendium cuts a wide swath across the several decades of commentary, and if there is one book to have for a representative sampling of what is out there, this is it. The very best of Jazz writing is here—how about Martin Williams, Stanley Crouch, Otis Ferguson, LeRoi Jones (Amiri Baraka), Gary Giddins, Dan Morgenstern, and Whitney Balliett for starters? There is no better pathway to the center of the wide world of Jazz writing than this collection.

The Reluctant Art: Five Studies in the Growth of Jazz, Benny Green: In some ways, Green was the English equivalent of Whitney Balliett—a superb stylist with a penchant for metaphor that illuminated, rather than darkened, the frequently murky waters of impressionistic criticism. He was also a professional saxophonist who brought to the page a thoroughly competent knowledge of the theoretical laws that undergird music. There are definitive essays on Bix Beiderbecke, Benny Goodman, Lester Young, Billie Holiday, and Charlie Parker that explore many unique facets of their music. This is one of the very best and least known Jazz books.

Sidney Bechet: The Wizard of Jazz, John Chilton: Bechet was one of the greatest of the Jazz originals, and arrived at his style before the advent of Armstrong. His story would make a phenomenal film, with its detours into jail, to Europe (where he introduced the true spirit of Jazz in 1919), to hard times during the Great Depression years (when he ran a tailor shop), to stardom in France during the last decade of his life. Trumpeter Chilton relates this wild life soberly, but nonetheless manages to keep you enthralled. He wisely chooses neither to embellish nor to underline—he leaves all the exclamation points to Bechet. Chilton's other biographies (Coleman Hawkins, Red Allen, Louis Jordan, and a new one on Roy Eldridge) are all of the same high quality.

Stomping the Blues, Albert Murray: This is one of the most original and (through Wynton Marsalis) influential books to have been written about the blues and how they spawned Jazz. From the get-go, Murray challenges all the clichés that have surrounded what the blues actually are and what their function in music and in life is. Murray's scope is so wide that it touches on virtually every aspect of our American life, and will lead you to his other definitive works, such as *The Omni-Americans* and *The Blue Devils of Nada* (which feature his two monumental essays on Armstrong and Ellington).

Swing Changes: Big-Band Jazz in New Deal America, David Stowe: One of the best attempts to place the Jazz of the 1930s within the social and cultural contexts. Stowe clearly has a good ear for the music and the overtones it strikes across musical and nonmusical boundaries. Not much in the way of musical analysis here, but that is more than compensated for by the insight the author brings to an era that answered severe challenges with a flowering of fine art.

The Swing Era: The Development of Jazz, 1930–1945, Gunther Schuller: As with his book *Early Jazz*, the sheer scope and depth of insight Schuller brings to bear on the music makes this tome truly indispensable. The only fault is that Schuller tends to be dismissive of artists who deserved a better shake (Bill Finegan and Benny Carter). But taken as a whole, there is nothing to compare with this. The bountiful musical examples are a boon to those who can read music, and an incentive to those who can't. The text works just as well, however, without being able to read the musical examples.

Swing to Bop, Ira Gitler: A lengthy and well-organized oral history tracing the evolution of Jazz from the '30s through the '40s. Gitler, a major Jazz writer since the '40s, knew just what to ask of whom, bringing to his writing an awareness of how musicians actually live and create that engendered replies that were different from the stock ones usually encountered. While the great figures—Young, Parker, and Gillespie—are dealt with in appropriate detail, there is an equal if not greater emphasis placed on the many players who made their own not inconsiderable, if largely overlooked, contributions such as Budd Johnson, Allen Tinney, Victor Coulson, and George Handy.

To Be or Not to Bop, Dizzy Gillespie: Gillespie, known for his clownlike exuberance on the bandstand, shows a far more analytical perspective as he tells his story with a disarming candor and leaves spaces for reminiscences from others that don't always jibe with his remembrance of things. The result is a sprawling and frequently touching picture of what many continue to call Jazz's golden age. Gillespie was one of the great teachers of Jazz (he showed hundreds of musicians how to do the things he had labored hard to create), and this need to analyze and explain serves him well as an author.

The Trouble with Cinderella, Artie Shaw: Shaw was the only major big-band leader (save Ellington) who had the literary chops to tell his own story. This was his first volume of autobiography, and it takes Shaw from his childhood in Connecticut, where he dealt with both his Jewish heritage and his devotion to Jazz, up toward the moment when he recorded "Begin the Beguine" and became an icon of American popular culture. In many ways, this is a story of his intellectual growth as seen through the prism of his musical career.

Visions of Jazz, Gary Giddins: An award-winning set of essays that cover the first one hundred years of Jazz. Giddins is a superb writer with an original voice that is at once challenging and inviting. The breadth of Giddins's enthusiasms is refreshing, as is his ability to engage the reader in that spirit without coming off as a cheerleader. Of particular interest is his original take on Al Jolson and other vocalists who emerged just as Jazz was evolving.

Magazines

Here is a list of Jazz magazines that do not have a major Internet presence. Virtually all of the best-known magazines have online editions (and can be found in the Websites section, below). There also some fine mags dedicated to specific instruments, with the *Saxophone Journal*, *Modern Drummer*, and *Bass Player* being among the best.

Cadence: Since the mid-seventies, this admittedly low-tech publication has covered the widest range of musicians (in extended interviews that frequently run in two parts), recordings, and publications of any magazine extant. It leans toward the avant-garde and its editorial slant may now seem a bit dated (keep at least a few doses of salt handy when reading), but these are minor issues. You will not find a better overview of the huge and sometimes messy world of Jazz than in this still homemade magazine that is so clearly a labor of love.

Jazz Improv: This quarterly magazine is hands down the best for the serious Jazz fan and for the professional musician. It is chock-full of in-depth interviews, high-quality transcriptions, and lead sheets. It also comes with an accompanying CD of the material discussed in the issue. While the range of music and styles covered is not as broad as it could be, it is nonetheless an undertaking that deserves much respect and which credits its readers with far more intelligence than they get at the hands of most of the other jazz publications.

Jazz Journal International: This English publication has a long and distinguished history and is now the major journal of record for "mainstream" jazz. It publishes lengthy interviews with musicians that the majors ignore, and many of them are quite wonderful (look for the mid-2001 issues with multi-instrumentalist Scott Robinson on the cover for the mag at its best). Some of the reviewers tend to be curmudgeons, but that comes with the territory. Each issue has much information you won't find anywhere else, including extended exchanges of historical and discographical data amongst its readers that is always interesting.

Websites

The number of interesting and well-constructed websites grows daily. Here are several that are informative and fun to use. Most of them have their own links page, which will shoot you off exponentially into Jazz cyberspace!

All About Jazz (allaboutJazz.com): This site is as good a place as you're going to find to keep a handle on what's new in Jazz these days. The level of the writing varies greatly, but there are extended sections on the local Jazz scenes all over the world, and an engaging sense that this site is run by people who actually care about the music and the musicians.

All Music Guide (allmusic.com): Writer Scott Yanow and his crew have picked up the slack from what Leonard Feather and George T. Simon did in the old days—reviewing all the new albums (complete with stars), writing bios, and creating a huge database of information, all of which is shared at this site. This is the best place to pick up personnel and reviews, but be wary of using it as a factual source—there are just enough errors to be dangerous.

Benny Carter Website (bennycarter.com): Born in 1907, Carter remains actively involved with music, and this website is the best way to keep tabs on him these days. Run by his close friends the Berger family, this site contains an intelligently formatted menu that includes photos, current CDs, and quotes and manages to represent the cool demeanor of its subject.

Dave Wild's WildPlace (home.att.net/~dawild): This major Jazz player and author is best known for his work on John Coltrane, and this site contains related items and more on Ornette Coleman. You will find all sorts of fascinating nuggets of information as you wend your way through what seems to be a relatively casual site. Wild is an excellent historian—if it's here, you can bank on it.

Downbeat (downbeat.com): The granddaddy (or, better yet, grandperson) of American Jazz mags is still going strong, and has recently made an editorial return to serious writing and engagement that is all the more remarkable given the status of Jazz in the commercial music and magazine worlds. As a website it is pretty basic, but does include more than enough reliable data and good writing to keep an intelligent surfer occupied.

Eric Dolphy Outward Bound (farcry.neurobio.pitt.edu/Eric.html): Dolphy was a ferociously original Jazzman (he played alto saxophone, bass clarinet, and flute) who mastered the tradition and then turned it inside out. He died young, and this site has many fascinating snippets of his work, in addition to a complete discography. Especially fascinating are the audio clips of a rare Dolphy interview—he sounds like a very mild-mannered chap—quite a contrast to his wild music!

Jazz at Lincoln Center (www.Jazzatlincolncenter.org): The best place to keep up on their varied doings in the world of Jazz, with educational pages and tour listings that can help you find them when they get close to your area. They are one of the few organizations that actually make an effort to reach out to their constituency, and they will follow up if you let them—try their feedback page!

JazzCorner (Jazzcorner.com): A site that lists many musicians' home pages, including their e-mail addresses and itineraries. There are also message boards here that frequently include posts by thoughtful people that are constructive and interesting.

JazzTimes (Jazztimes.com): While the magazine's literary standards are uneven (the CD reviews in particular range from A to Z in terms of basic literary and critical skills), this is one of the bedrocks of the business. Though there are the short puff pieces that reek of promotion, they will still, on occasion, print extended and substantive ones, but these remain the exception rather than the rule. Having said that, their website is quite good, and if you know where the wheat is, you can easily bypass the chaff.

Jelly Roll Morton (doctorJazz.freeserve.co.uk/page10.html): A detailed trek through the life of one of Jazz's greatest composers and blowhards. The site is loaded with links upon links that wend their way to virtually every corner of his life. Though Morton died in 1941, there have been major breakthroughs in the story of his life in recent years which are reflected here. This is a great website to get lost in!

Mike Fitzgerald Home Page (eclipse.net/~fitzgera/): If this country had a greater sense of its cultural worth, a person like Mike Fitzgerald (who is a high school music teacher) would be given a position somewhere to do his good work. Said work is Jazz historical scholarship of the highest level, and for years now Mike's website has been the gateway to the best of the new Jazz research. He only includes links that he feels are worthy.

NPR Jazz (nprJazz.org): A wide array of reviews, interviews, and general information is available here. Especially useful is their state by state listing of stations that carry NPR programming (and a number of NPR stations still preserve a Jazz format)—anyone who has been on the road knows how important finding an intelligent voice on the radio can be.

Red Hot Jazz Archive (redhotJazz.com): This site is nothing short of astounding—literally hundreds of pre-WWII Jazz recordings are streamable in their entirety, in above average sound. You can search by musician or band name, and there is usually an excellent biography to go along with it. For those who want to truly understand the miracles that Armstrong, Morton, Ellington, and the other Jazz giants of the era wrought, you have to immerse yourself in the sounds from which they emerged, and this is the place to do it.

Solo Flight: The Charlie Christian Website (home.elp.rr.com/valdes/): Guitarist Leo Valdes has put together this fount of useful information about guitarist Christian, whose influence has proved to be as long-lived as he himself was short-lived. You will find a detailed discography, with attention paid to new discoveries and releases, and many transcriptions of Christian solos, many of which are from rare recordings. There is also a photo gallery that contains many unpublished items.

William Gottlieb's Photographs from the Golden Age of Jazz (memory.loc.gov/ammem/wghtml/wghome.html): Gottlieb took many of the music's most famous photographs during the years surrounding the Second World War. They were acquired by the Library of Congress, which has made virtually all of them available for viewing. Even shots that are well known are supplemented by uncropped and alternate versions—a lesser known but essential site.

Documentaries

Good films about Jazz are few and far between. Even the most well-intentioned filmmakers, including Clint Eastwood, Woody Allen, and Bernard Tavernier, in their feature-length films have yet to transcend the clichés and distortions that color how most people in the world view the music and its makers. Here are some items that, though dealing with music from quite awhile ago, remain fresher and more truthful than any number of more recent attempts to represent the music.

A Great Day in Harlem, Jean Bach, dir.: Though it runs only an hour, it packs so much life, humor, and insight into every one of its sixty minutes that it's hard to believe it is so short. Wonderfully edited and content to let the viewers do some thinking for themselves, this film tells the story of the famous 1958 *Esquire* photo shoot in Harlem that gathered together for the only time dozens of Jazz's towering figures. Imagine seeing Count Basie, Thelonious Monk, Sonny Rollins, Bud Freeman, Lester Young, Pee Wee Russell, Art Blakcy, and Miff Mole hanging out on the same doorstep! With rare home-movie footage and revealing interviews, this documentary tells the real story of these musicians and how their music reflected their lives.

Jammin' the Blues, Gjon Mili, dir.: The first artistic short film on Jazz, made in Hollywood by the photographer Gjon Mili, remains unsurpassed in its evocation of the spirit of the music. It caught Lester Young, Sid Catlett, and Harry Edison in 1944 at the height of their powers, and although there are moments where they are ever so slightly out of sync with the pre-recorded soundtrack, just to see them and their playing attitudes is pure magic.

Jazz, Ken Burns, dir.: Loved by the masses and torn apart in a dysfunctional fashion by the Jazz community, the mammoth undertaking tells the story of race in America, as did Burns's previous shows on baseball and the Civil War. Though it is broken up into several episodes, which work as self-contained units, the best way to really view it is from beginning to end. Through expert editing and a riveting narrative, Burns found a way to capture the imaginations of the uninitiated.

The Last of the Blue Devils, Bruce Ricker, dir.: Ricker has the prescience to gather as many of the founding fathers of Kansas City Jazz in their later years for a one-time only reunion and to film it with any eye toward capturing both the human foibles and the sheer transcendent musical majesty of his subjects. For every world-famous KC graduate (Count Basie, Big Joe Turner, Eddie Durham, Jay McShann) there is a local talent who also had a hand in creating the magic—Fiddler Claude Williams, who had a whole new career based on this appearance; the drummer Baby Lovett; and any number of lesser figures. There is as much humor to be found here as there is swing, and once again, the Ophulslike breadth of Ricker's technique renders his subjects in startling detail. There is a good amount of new and worthwhile footage in this DVD reissue.

The Sound of Jazz, Jack Smight, dir.: This CBS television show was broadcast live in December 1957 and contains many of the greatest Jazz moments ever captured on film. The producer, Robert Herridge, brought in two leading critics, Nat Hentoff and Whitney Balliett, as consultants to make sure that the right musicians were hired and that they were set in the best context. He then instructed Smight to have his cameramen get the best shot at any given moment, regardless of whether there was another camera in the way. It is sobering to think of an assemblage of this magnitude (a partial— yes, partial—listing would include Pee Wee Russell, Thelonious Monk, Gerry Mulligan, Count Basie, Lester Young, Ben Webster, Roy Eldridge, Coleman Hawkins, and Billie Holiday). Unlike films, television allowed them to play live, and they reacted to the natural setting with nothing short of brilliance. Available on video, this may be the one Jazz item to have before all others.

Straight, No Chaser, Charlotte Zwerin, dir.: Years after it was shot and its subject had died, a treasure trove of footage of Thelonious Monk was discovered. With Eastwood's backing, it was turned into a very moving, mature, and music-filled documentary about one of the music's most humorous (purposefully) and brilliant innovators. Director Charlotte Zwerin skillfully intersperses new interviews with the '60s footage, and creates a cinematic tonality entirely consonant with that of Monk's music. She pulls no punches when it comes to dealing with Monk's mental problems, which exacted a toll on his family and friends, but the tone here is one of respect and is miles away from even a whiff of exploitation.

Index